SECOND AMERICAN EDITION
Published in 2012 by Futility Press LLC.

LIBRARY OF CONGRESS CATALOGING-IN-PUBLICATION DATA

Ben-Caro, Yared M.
Dreidel Full of LEAD: From the Wild West to the Streets of Gaza/
by SSgt. Yared M. Ben-Caro

ISBN-13: 978-0984964802
ISBN-10: 0984964800

1. Israel Defense Force 2. Operation: Cast Lead 3. Israeli Paratroopers 4. Israel. 5. Hamas 6. Israeli-Palestinian Conflict. 7. Gaza. 8. Arab-Israeli Conflict. 9. Terrorism 10. Ben-Caro, Yared M.

DEDICATED TO:

WO Lutfi Nasereldeen
SSgt. Dvir Emanuelof
Cpl. Yousef Moadi
Maj. (Dr.) Dagan Whartman
SSgt. Nitai Stern
Cpt. Yoni Netanel
SSgt. Alex Mashevitsky
Maj. Roi Rozner
Sgt. Amit Rubinson
Cpt. Omer Rubinovich

*and all of the other fallen and wounded Soldiers of the Israel Defense Force
who fought in Operation: Cast Lead*

I still remember "The Last Dance"

SPECIAL THANKS TO:

My fellow Paratroopers, particularly my partner designated marksmen, "Axl" and
"Lunchbox." As "Axl" always used to quote:
*"We few, we happy few, we band of brothers. For he today that sheds his blood with me shall be
my brother." -- "Henry V" by William Shakespeare*

"Rocky-Roodle," who never ceased to give me a reason to smile when we were together
during my military service. Even though "It's Been Awhile"
I still play our song and remember:
*"In your house I long to be / Room by room, patiently / I'll wait for you there, like a stone /
I'll wait for you there, alone / Alone." -- "Like A Stone" by Audioslave*

My adoptive family on my kibbutz, especially Avram S., who is one of the most inspiring
individuals that I have ever been privileged enough to meet and whose entire family is held in
my very highest admiration and affection.

All of my friends during my military service, in particular "Toohey," "Rio," and "Reaper,"
who all gave me much needed distractions at every opportunity
from the harsh realities I faced daily.

Chana W., Dovid Z., and all of the staff of Chabad.org for all of the hard work and dedication
put into my blog and the original and highly abridged version of this work.

Friends of the IDF for all of their generosity that I received throughout my military service.

Rabbi Shmuel T., who gave me my first opportunities to speak publicly about my experiences
on the front lines and consistently encouraged me in my efforts to write this book and support
the soldiers of the Israel Defense Force.

Tzvi T., the aforementioned rabbi's son, who probably had this entire manuscript memorized
before publication simply because he never tired of begging me to tell him repeatedly *all* of my
"army stories." And to his poor mother, Chana T., who was quite often a captive audience.

Dr. Roselin "Tempe" Reiss for many hours of painstaking editing.

"Nilla Pride" for the inspiration of the name of this book.

Liliana "LIFE" Elkouss for the cover design

Constantin Raducan for the "About the Author" photograph

And my best friend "DJ," who always eagerly listened to the accounts of my adventures and
escapades, even on the occasions that I suspected he grew weary of my rambling.

THE TOP TEN LESSONS I HAVE LEARNED IN LIFE:

10. *Never underestimate the potential depravity of the human being.*

9. *Don't be overly concerned about an issue that will affect you
   for less than twenty-four hours.*

8. *Being feared is an acceptable substitute for being respected.*

7. *People don't believe the truth. People believe what they want to believe.*

6. *The greatest of all crimes is betrayal.*

5. *Women are often emotionally unstable and protected by the double-standards of society.
   Therefore they can be dangerous. Proceed with caution.*

4. *There is no substitute for total victory. If you are confident in the cause
   that you are fighting for, destroy your enemy mercilessly.*

3. *If you treat everyone you meet with respect, ninety percent of the world will reciprocate.*

2. *Take calculated risks. Never allow yourself to be asked,
   "What would have happened if…"*

1. *Live every day so that tomorrow you can look at yourself in the mirror,
   be proud of who you are, and have a great story tell.*

Map of Israel and the Conflict

CONTENTS

INTRODUCTION

He likewise had been standing too close to the exploded gas grenade and also vacated the area, although his retreat was significantly more dignified.

Although I studied physics in high school and university I unfortunately didn't apply my learning to the current situation. All of these events occurred as we were sleeping on a small hill. I fled from the grenade by running *up* the hill. The problem was that most gases rise. So in my desperate attempt to escape the searing pain I merely entered the CS cloud itself and gassed myself even more. I simply continued to run, knowing that eventually I would get out of the gas cloud. I ran so far my platoon commander, soon to be called Lieutenant Gold, had to come find me.

Apparently this was how the Israeli army woke up their soldiers at three in the morning.

Monday:

One facet of the exercises was that we were not allowed to urinate in the field. They gave us a one and a half liter bottle and told us to urinate in that. The idea was that the enemy could track us if we left urine and other remains behind. At least, that was the theory. I didn't quite understand it myself. This was also the only exercise where we were required to do this.

The point of this week was to practice moving in fighting formation up and down hills, set up ambushes, etc. The main difficulties arose from fatigue because we were not eating well, sleeping well, and had at least fifty pounds (twenty-three kilograms) on our backs at all times. At first it wasn't so bad. The problem was that we did not stop at all for four days. It was so hot that I sometimes felt as if I had joined an army in the Middle East. The commanders didn't let us stop or quit, even if we were sick or injured. I soon realized that I was going to come out of this week hurt in some way. Knowing I was probably going to be physically damaged and was simply wondering how severe was a very unpleasant feeling for someone who was new in the military. The fact that I would for sure need to see the medic afterward and possibly even go to the hospital had obviously negative mental connotations. It was very strange to watch the effects on people psychologically. Some of the best soldiers completely freaked out, losing themselves in a state of panic.

After a full day of exercises we were standing in formation at about eleven o'clock at night. Our platoon-commanding officer, Lieutenant Gold, was giving us a briefing and received a call on his cell phone. He stepped away momentarily, which was a fairly normal occurrence. One of the officer's

Hummers was meandering around the area. It passed by our formation at a swift speed. Out of nowhere our insane captain leaned out of the window of the Hummer and threw yet another gas grenade into the formation. It exploded. Something hot and metallic hit me in the face and cut my lip a little. Then I heard the ominous hissing of the gas. And again I ran like hell. But so did everybody else this time.

More than once we wondered if our captain was a lunatic. He previously served in a top-notch commando unit and switched to our division because of better promotion opportunities. But sometimes we questioned his mental state. Regardless, as a warrior his skill and training were legendary. [1]

Tuesday:

It was afternoon. The heat from the Middle Eastern sun beat down on us unrelentlessly. and I opened up my large bag to bring out another bottle of water because it was just so unbearably hot. As I began to rummage through my supplies I was dismayed to discover that one of my water bottles had burst.

But then I realized that it wasn't water and erupted into a long string of profanity.

It was urine.

Apparently my urine bottle had burst inside my bag. Not only were all my clothes and equipment soaked in urine, but my Bar Mitzvah set of *tallit* (prayer shawl) and *tefillin* (small boxes attached to the forehead and arm for prayer) were ruined. The *tallit* I could probably wash but I had little hope for the *tefillin*. [1]

[1 According to rumor heard later, Captain Gasman apparently was making his way back to the special forces front lines. The story circulating was that he had been involved in a counter-terrorist operation in which his best friend had been shot near Shechem (Nablus). Captain Gasman tried to get him out, running and carrying him to safety. Tragically, the wounded soldier died in his arms. Not long after Captain Gasman took a break and was working as a non-commissioned officer in logistics. Ultimately he wanted to get back into the action and being the commanding-captain of our company-in-training was the stepping stone. After we finished training he was promoted to the captain in charge of *Duv-Devan*, one of the most infamous counter-terrorism commando units in the world. For us as brand-new recruits, however, we got the shock of our lives under his supervision.]

It was another full day of exercises. At the end of the day we were situated on a hill in ambush position and our insane commanding officer, now known as Captain Gasman, conducted exercises in the valley below. Out of the darkness of the valley he shot something green right at me on the hill. I watched the green fiery orb arc through the air and begin its decent towards me. I grabbed my equipment and once again ran like the devil. A few minutes later Corporal Unibrow laughed and asked me why I was afraid of a flare.

"You know what," I responded to his ridicule. "First of all I have never seen a green flare before. All the flares we've used so far have been orange. Secondly if there's one thing I've learned this week it's that when I see an unidentified flying object coming my way I don't wait around to find out what it is."[2]

After an incessant series of other training activities we marched all night with over fifty pounds (twenty-three kilograms) on our backs for almost ten miles. Again, being the first real experience in the field, I definitely was beginning to feel the effects.

[1 To this day I am famous for this story. My commanders would not stop talking about it and reminding me of it for my entire service, and even after. It was even the featured story in the "Year Book," so to speak, of our draft. Also, the military rabbi later sent me home to my religious kibbutz to have my *tefillin* checked by a *sefer stam* (a specialist in Jewish holy writings) to determine if they were still "kosher" and usable. I really didn't think this examination was necessary. I was sure that somewhere in *Halachah* (traditional Jewish law) it was written that *tefillin* drenched and stinking of rotting urine were not fit for use. I later had to explain to the *sefer stam* what happened to them. I responded lamely that they had gotten wet.

"How?" He asked jokingly. "Did you go to the beach wearing them?"

"Um, not exactly. A funny thing happened to me in the IDF Paratroopers involving a bottle of urine..."]

[2 My commanders and officers were particularly enthralled with ridiculing me with this story as well. They were so impressed by this incident, in fact, that "Green Flare" later became an informal code in Paratroopers 890 for anything dangerous, particularly an incoming explosive.]

Wednesday:

After a full march and all the insanity of the week we finally returned to our base that morning. We had gone the entire night without sleep and we were exhausted. The commanders were nice enough to give us a good barbecue-style meal, but then they put us to work the whole day organizing and cleaning equipment. I then examined my "scars of battle." It actually wasn't as bad as I had feared. The main complaint was my feet. My whole left foot was covered with blisters. I had a massive blister on my heel. I punctured it with the tip of a knife and an actual stream of water shot out. I also had a huge blister on my toe that started bleeding and became infected. The army medic took one look at my feet and exclaimed, "Whoa, that's really bad." That definitely was not a good sign. But I knew in the end I would be okay. Besides, I had been expecting worse.

October 13th, 2007: Designated Marksman

The Israel Defense Force had noticed my ability to shoot and almost immediately decided to put me through the special training required to become a sharpshooter, or designated marksman. I was given a new M4 rifle (which was similar to the short M16 but boasted several improvements, particularly the rifling of the barrel and the option of customizing sights and scopes), a daytime scope and a specialized night vision scope. Needless to say I was quite pleased. Even better was the fact that I would later be given an opportunity to take the sniper's course.

As it was, I could load my assault rifle, drop to the ground, pop out my bi-pod stand, and take the head off of a terrorist from over one thousand feet (three hundred meters) away in only a few seconds. Yes, it was an amazing feeling to know that I was becoming more lethal by the day.

One of the logistic sergeants had given me a special "reward," if you will. Essentially he maintained the responsibility of ensuring that the barracks and the equipment of our unit were in order. Accordingly, the lower-ranking soldiers took turns helping him out in his daily work. He apparently was so fond of working with me he gave me public recognition and always requested my assistance with any special tasks he had. On the one hand, I guess I had unintentionally made myself "the sergeant's slave." But on the other hand a pat on the back and a "job well done" was something that I had always appreciated. I soon realized, however, that being a favorite of the logistic sergeants had more downsides than perks.

Much more important, however, Lieutenant Gold had selected me to be *mitztayan* of basic training for our platoon. *"Mitztayan"* was a term used for a soldier who had proved himself to be worthy of special recognition. We completed a nine mile fast march loaded up with all of our equipment. At the end of the march we trudged on an additional two miles carrying soldiers on stretchers. At the end of this march we received our Paratrooper insignias. They were similar to a patch but could be more accurately described as a rubber/plastic tag hanging down our shoulder from a lapel.

I stood there paying little attention, wishing our lieutenant would just hurry up his speech. He was just rambling on about how great somebody was, that he was so motivated, never complained, was willing to do anything they told him to, was here by choice rather than mandatory draft, etc.

"Okay, whatever, I just want to eat, shower, and go to sleep," I thought to myself as the officer droned on.

"Killswitch, come on up here."

I came back to reality glanced around me briefly, in shock that he said my name, wondering at first if I understood the Hebrew correctly or if there were any other crazy Americans named Killswitch in my unit of the Paratroopers. I stepped forward to receive the tag. It was Lieutenant Gold's own tag. He personally signed it and wrote me his wishes for success.[1] It was a huge honor and it definitely made my week.

There was a special position in my unit that I really wanted. Lieutenant Gold needed to pick one designated marksman to become something like his "combat assistant." The idea was that when we had any kind of mission I would stick close to the lieutenant and take out mid-range targets at his command. If we needed to raid a house and kick the door in we would go in first together. I had previously met someone who was given this task and he emphasized how much he liked it. I wanted to request this position but I wasn't sure how to go about it. The first step was for me to become a designated marksman, which I had already accomplished. Not long after a different officer asked me if I had ever heard about this position and if I wanted it. My response to both questions was a resounding "Yes." He told me he would relay this message to my officers and commanders. But ultimately the decision was up to Lieutenant Gold, the same lieutenant who had designated me as *mitztayan* and given me his personal insignia. He was a twenty-two year old religious Jew like me. Honestly I think we would have been good friends if we didn't have rank separating us.[2]

The other day I met a beautiful Sephardic Israeli girl on a bus. It didn't take long for me to get her phone number. We later met up and went to the beach in Tel Aviv in the middle of the night. By "coincidence" she happened to have a blanket in the backseat of her car. She was only twenty and thought she was being slick. I knew better but played along. I wasn't stupid. There on the beach we sat and talked and drank a few beers. As the quiet conversation drifted from

[1] This tag was later stolen by someone who replaced it with the similar tag but with a different personal message. The other personal message was a love note from some army secretary to some soldier. I was highly irritated. But the name of the soldier had worn off so I couldn't retaliate.]

[2] We still keep in touch to this day.]

topic to topic I mentioned my brother and his family briefly.

"Are you jealous of your brother?" She asked me, her beautiful dark eyes glistening in the moonlight.

I stopped and looked around me. There I was, sitting on the beach with a beer in one hand and a beautiful Israeli girl in the other. My M4 assault rifle and uniform lay in the trunk of her car. The cool night breeze playfully danced in her long dark hair and the smell of Mediterranean Sea air filled my nostrils.

"Am I jealous?" I repeated rhetorically, as I ran my fingers through her long hair and leaned in close for a kiss. "No, I really don't think so..."

October 20th, 2007: Chicken Stealing

For four days we conducted training operations in the field. We went out to practice a specific charging maneuver. But we only had enough practice planned to last for a day and a half. To fill the time the officers supplemented a makeshift training program that seemed rather senseless. And after four days of purposeless training in the heat I started to get annoyed.

Afterwards they called for an equipment preparation and inspection that should have taken about three to four hours at the most. Somehow it took our commanders and officers twenty-two hours to allow us to properly prepare our equipment and have it inspected. We went the whole night without sleep again for absolutely no reason.

And I, the perfect angel of the army, or so they thought, almost lost my weekend leave three times. What were my heinous crimes that I had to talk my way out of?

First we had been in the field for most of the week. When we were in the field we ate the Israeli version of C-rations. We were consistently given a box whose contents were a few cans of tuna, *Loof* (the kosher version of Spam), a can of corn, a can of pickles, a few packages of chocolate spread, and bread. This had been breakfast, lunch, and dinner for four days. Our officers somehow failed to mention to the dining room our impending return to the base from the field. Thus when we returned to the base they continued to give us these boxes of cans to eat for our meals. At lunch time my friend from Philadelphia, Lunchbox, noticed that they were serving a high-quality broiled chicken in the dining room which we were apparently not entitled to eat. So my friend came up with a not-so-cleverly devised plan to steal some. We actually would have gotten away with it if some other soldiers from our group hadn't gotten the same idea and blown our cover. We had infiltrated the dining room from a back entrance, acquired the food, and had strategically placed ourselves in a corner with low exposure. But then two other soldiers did the same thing but came in through the front entrance and sat right next to the door. Sure enough they were seen and caught. Lunchbox and I immediately evacuated, leaving the food trays and made a break for the door. We made it out but immediately thereafter Commander Unibrow demanded to know what we were doing in the dining hall. We had to do some quick talking and get ourselves out of that one. I was pretty sure we had succeeded.

However, we didn't leave the dining room empty handed. We had dropped several large, juicy, greasy chicken breasts into the pockets of our dusty, sweaty, muddy uniforms. We made our way to the *beit knesset* (synagogue) and devoured them in the corner.

It was delicious.

The second major incident that almost caused me to lose my weekend pass involved leaving the base. Lone Soldiers like me were Israeli soldiers, usually *olim chadashim* (new immigrants), who were entitled to extra privileges due to the fact that we served without any assistance from immediate family. One such privilege was receiving an extra day off every other month to run errands and otherwise manage our personal affairs. There was a bus that left from the base at seven every morning. Our corporals gave me and Lunchbox very distinct instructions on where to go after our twenty-four hour leave because of a special guard assignment coming up. They told us to switch into our dress uniforms and that we would be taking the seven o'clock bus. Apparently they didn't actually want us to just take the bus and leave, even though that would be the obvious implication. It was true that normally an officer needed to talk to us before we left to make sure we knew when to return to base, to be safe with our rifles (because we took them home), and essentially not to be drunken fools. But since the corporals had talked to us about most of these details and said nothing about having *another* pre-exit briefing we started to leave to take the bus. We made it all the way to the bus stop just ten minutes before the bus left and my cell phone started ringing. It was Commander Unibrow. He was very upset that we left without the "proper" pre-exit briefing. So we had to run all the way back, listen to Lieutenant Gold chew us out like little kids for not following what to him was "obvious" protocol, and he quite obviously tried to make us miss the bus. The next bus wasn't for almost three hours. Whenever we had a briefing with an officer the corporals *always* told us. This time they didn't and gave the briefing themselves, or so we thought. Besides, they themselves didn't even realize the mistake until eight minutes before the bus left which was ridiculous because of time it took to trek to the bus stop after the briefing. They clearly had made a mistake and just wanted to blame us instead.

In the designated marksmen we had a new slogan. The hit movie about the Spartans, *300*, was quite popular in Israel at that time. Most famous was the scene in which the Spartan commander yelled, "Men of Sparta, what is your profession?" And the soldiers responded with guttural cheering. We had somehow adopted this as the slogan of the designated marksmen. I would commence the shouting in English with the Israelis cheering in reply. Yes, it was rather strange and quite cheesy, I know.

The IDF had acquired from the Americans a wide collection of used uniforms, such as the green camouflage fatigues. Israel normally used plain olive uniforms.

When I asked why we did not utilize a more sophisticated form of camouflage I was informed that, while snipers often used different uniforms, the olive green was actually usually better camouflage than the green-euro patterns. Also the green-euro uniforms were too similar to the Syrian uniforms. Thus we had stuck with plain olive green uniforms almost identical to the American uniform used in Vietnam. On a side note, the American Euro-pattern uniforms were used for training, and the desert uniforms somehow became the dress of soldiers currently serving time in various "military jails." I had a sneaking suspicion that the real reason we didn't have better uniforms was simply because we were cheap. After all, this was the army of the Jewish people. Likewise, we only put twenty-nine bullets into a thirty bullet magazine. Supposedly it was less stress on the spring mechanisms inside. I personally felt it was because someone in the accounting office realized that by dropping just one bullet per magazine in the long run they would save a lot of money.

These uniforms still brandished "US ARMY" on them. Correspondingly, I took a permanent marker and wrote "Under New Management" above it.

When a person was situated on a military base for long periods of time and didn't get out into the real world he slowly lost his sanity a little bit at a time. More than that, I personally found little ways to amuse myself. My recently found hobby was stealing. No, I had not become a thief of wallets or cell phones. I had made a fascinating discovery recently. The base was under constant supervision by somebody, usually fellow soldiers in basic training. I realized that it was great fun to try to steal worthless objects without being spotted by the guards. For instance, Paratrooper unit and division flags hung scattered throughout the barracks. It became my personal hobby to get up in the middle of the night, sneak past the guards, stealthily cut down the flags, and make my daring escape. In the morning I would overhear the logistics sergeants complain about the disappearing flags. They never suspected that their perfect little "pet" was responsible.1

I was most proud, however, of the fact that I actually broke into the *Neshkiah* (the locked and guarded gun warehouse, or armory) and stole a poster from off the wall. I departed, leaving the empty frame hanging desolately on the wall.

This had become my life. I had resorted to snatching chicken for survival and lifting flags for entertainment. Regardless, the Israeli military was not easy. It was beyond doubt quite a difficult lifestyle, but I wouldn't have had it any other way.

[1 I got bored easily, what can I say?]

October 24th, 2007: Psychological Warfare

It soon became a necessity to write personal slogans and draw unique logos on our equipment to make sure no one else "accidentally" took it. And sometimes a soldier's name or initials simply weren't enough. Eventually, due to an incessant problem with missing equipment, I found my only solution was to draw a Confederate States of America flag on all of my property. I wasn't a racist by any means. But I had family in the South and my ancestors had supported the Rebel cause. Most importantly, the "stars and bars" flag bore absolutely no resemblance to any other logo or design in the IDF. It was only then that my personal equipment stopped disappearing.

I had heard that Nine Inch Nails would soon be coming to Tel Aviv, but I had to figure out how to get out of the army to go. Ironically, the opening band for NIN was a British alternative metal band called "Unkle." So I came up with a brilliant plan.

"As you know I am a lone soldier," I addressed my officers and the female social worker assigned to me in the military. "There are some people coming to Israel that are very important to me that I haven't seen in over two years. (This statement was actually true because the last time NIN was on tour in the United States had been two years before). And they even have my "Unkle" with them. And family is very important to me since my mother passed away. They are having a get-together, if you will, with a lot of people, food, and even a little bit of alcohol. It's really important for me to go."

"Oh, we think we can give you the night off for that."

Later Lieutenant Gold and the social worker informed me that, due to my excellent performance, they had not just given me the Thursday night off. They had given me a three-day weekend pass.

Yes, I had used my dead mother to go see a rock concert and I was destined for hell.

We had an American in our unit from Los Angeles. He had since received the nickname "WD-40." He was a slick, oily flirt that somehow managed to get away with *everything*. WD-40 was also a ridiculously successful player. I couldn't deny he was physically built and very good looking. However, as we prepared to go into the field on a training exercise he began confiding in me.

"You know, Killswitch, I don't know what I'm becoming. I have this unnatural ability to lie and manipulate girls and I don't know where it's going to lead. But I just can't stop."

"I don't know, WD." I answered facetiously. "I tried being honest with girls and gave up. I went back to lying and it works a lot better." Obviously I wasn't serious but apparently WD-40 was.

"Yeah, that's what my dad said, too," WD-40 smiled as we lay on our backs looking at the stars. We were waiting for the rest of our company to meet us at the rendezvous point to continue a nocturnal training exercise. "That's why my parents are married. Because men lie and women are stupid enough to believe our lies. That's what makes the world go 'round."[1]

[[1] This philosophy would soon come back to bite WD-40 badly. He soon came down with a vicious STD that would cause him severe health issues throughout his military service.]

November 2nd, 2007: They Bombed Themselves?

They sent me and my company of Paratroopers to a Jewish "settlement" just a few kilometers outside of Shechem (also known as "Nablus" in Arabic.) Shechem was a city that had been in existence for four thousand years. This was the city that Yaakov's (Jacob's) two sons, Shimon and Levi, destroyed in direct retaliation to the king's son raping and kidnapping their sister, Dinah. It was also near Shiloh, the place that the *Mishkan*, or Tabernacle, rested for over four hundred years before King Solomon built the Temple. Now it was an Arab city and one of the most terrorist-saturated places in the world. It always seemed ironic to me that the long history of Jewish civilization and corresponding archeology were completely ignored on the political spectrum. Most of these areas claimed absolutely no long-term Arab civilization, or any significant Arab civilization at all before the advent of the British Empire in the Palestine Mandate in 1917. And these areas were now considered by many to be "stolen Palestinian Arab lands" and "occupied territories."

Shechem and the outskirt villages were situated in a bowl-shaped valley. On the rims of the mountains surrounding these Arab villages were a handful of Jewish villages populated by religious and very Zionistic Jews. The Israeli military protected the Jews living in the villages and also used them as a place to base reconnaissance and Intel-gathering operations.

It was my duty to stand on the mountain in various guard posts about a quarter mile (half of a kilometer) from the Arab villages below. I was so close I actually watched an Arab wedding take place on a rooftop with my binoculars.

We brushed up on a few Arabic phrases, particularly one that began with *"Wakif." "Wakif"* was a term that meant to stop in the context of surrendering and submitting and was part of a sentence that could be translated as "Stop and surrender or you will be fired upon."

One fine Shabbat morning I was guarding and caught sight of someone in flowing white clothing gaily tripping along toward my post. There was an official "No-Man's-Land" between the Jewish settlement and the Arab village, although technically it belonged to the Jewish settlement. This quarter mile (half kilometer) area was designed as a buffer zone between the Jews and the Arabs. There was absolutely no reason for anyone to be wandering around in it, Jew or Arab. I had orders to stop anyone in this area at gunpoint.

This person came along and I jumped down behind a rock and waited for him to approach. What was that Arabic phrase I was supposed to yell? *"Wakif"* something-or-rather. He found a hole in the barbed wire and continued to near me. As he drew closer I noticed that he was wearing a *kippah* (yarmulke, or Jewish head covering) and *tallit* (prayer shawl) and therefore at least he looked Jewish. I popped out and shouted *"Atzur"* ("Stop" in Hebrew) and put up my hand to indicate that he should immediately halt. He saw me with my hand out.

"Shabbat shalom! (Peaceful Sabbath)" He cheerfully greeted me, apparently thinking that my outstretched hand was waving at him.

"No, Stop!" I shouted and pointed the gun at him, thinking to myself, *"I put my hand out telling you to stop, you idiot, not to wish you a good morning."*

I talked to him for a few minutes and confirmed that he was just out for a Shabbat morning stroll through a barbed-wired area separating him from terrorists. I felt rather bad about it later, though, because apparently he was always extremely hospitable to the soldiers, routinely giving us coffee and chocolate. I felt kind of guilty taking his coffee later. I don't know if I would have been so nice to someone if he had almost shot me.

Almost every day the Israeli F-15 Eagles buzzed the terrorist-filled valley. They had a tactic of coming in low, hitting the afterburners, and then pulling out, creating a massive sonic boom that bounced half a dozen times throughout the valley. The effect was priceless. In the valley the terrorists hunkered down in their residences, knowing that the Israeli government wanted them dead. Then they would hear an enemy fighter jet and stop their bomb-making or machine gun-loading to see what would happen with baited breath. Waiting... Waiting... and then *BOOM!* The whole house shook and the windows rattled from the sonic boom. That had to have scared them to death.

Apparently, however, the terrorists had gotten tired of this tactic. One day I was at my guard duty post watching this routine. And the terrorists apparently were at their wits' end. They actually took Kassam non-guided rockets and launched two of them in the ridiculous hope of hitting the jets flying overhead. Obviously they didn't even come close, but I guess the retaliation attempt made them feel better. But what happened when they fired a non-guided rocket straight up into the air? What goes up must come down. The rocket eventually fell back down into the bowl-shaped valley below on top of their Arab neighbors.

There was a Givati Battalion on call at the time conducting Hummer patrols. I listened to their intense conversation on the radio.

"I just heard a large explosion. What happened?"

"They fired Kassams into the air."

"At what? What did they bomb?"

"Um... Themselves."

"What? Did you say they just bombed themselves?"

"Yes, sir."[1]

Two years before this the most exciting thing that happened in my life was getting into a drunken fight at a Rob Zombie concert. Oh, the places that life took me.

After the guarding assignment in Shechem we returned to our Paratrooper base. The following week we continued our training exercises in the field. It was a rather difficult week. The training was quite intense but some of the exercises we conducted I actually really enjoyed, particularly setting up night ambushes against out fellow soldiers who acted as "enemies" and shooting blanks at each other.

It was now the end of basic training and I was moving on to advanced training. To signify the end of basic training we embarked on a five mile (nine kilometer) march carrying stretchers for the entire duration. To show enthusiasm we all smeared on camouflage make up. Even better, at the end of the march when we returned to base one of the officers pulled me aside and told me, "Do your thing." So I stepped out in front of the soldiers and shouted,

[1] The Palestinian Arabs later complained heavily to the United Nations about the Israeli jets, turning it into an international incident. However, one should keep in mind that when terrorists intentionally surrounded themselves with civilians and non-combatants, the civilians inevitably suffered. This was true everywhere regardless of the nation or army. It was also a violation of the Geneva Convention and even a war crime, which somehow never seemed to be remembered when various governments and organizations criticized the Israel Defense Force. It should also be noted that it seemed a bit hypocritical for the United Nations to be concerned with momentary noise pollution in Yehudah V' Shomron (the West Bank) and to have done little to nothing about over three hundred thousand people who have been slaughtered in the Darfur region of Sudan for no other reason than the black color of their skin.]

77

"Battalion 890! What is your profession?!"

They all responded with their Spartan war grunts. Then they gave me the Israeli flag to carry and lead the Paratroopers back to base.

PART IV: ADVANCED TRAINING

November 14th, 2007: Education Epidemic

These past two weeks we first participated in something called "Education Week." It consisted of a series of classes on the history of Israel, the army, and other such related topics. Unfortunately, many of the eighteen year-old kids still thought they were in high school which highly annoyed me. Sometimes I must admit that it was quite hard being in the army because I was so much older than everyone else. I was a month away from my twenty-third birthday and everyone else was only eighteen years old, maybe nineteen. That caused a collection of obvious problems. I was simply not a stupid eighteen year-old kid. Accordingly, their perception was that I was just a boring goody-good because I didn't disrespect the officers like they did or pull the same immature antics. It was kind of ironic that anyone would ever call me a goody-good, especially considering how much chicken and how many flags I had already stolen.

Afterwards we went on a brief tour of the Old City of Jerusalem. Our company of about sixty soldiers crammed the narrow alleyways observing the sights and sounds of the ancient city. Suddenly a very attractive Arab girl with a Moslem head covering walked through our cluster of Paratroopers. It was one of those moments when I thought to myself, "You know, she's actually really cute. This is weird that I'm thinking this about an Arab girl while I'm in my IDF uniform." Apparently I wasn't alone in the sentiment. As she passed by I heard a certain Ethiopian-Jewish soldier chime in a saucy and suggestive undertone, *"Wakif, Wakif,"* referring to the Arabic phrase for "Stop and surrender."

We all broke out into laughter. She rolled her eyes in disgust and kept on walking.

"What do you think you're you doing?!" One of our corporals, Commander Snoopy, yelled at him, doing his best not to start laughing himself.

"Um, you know... Just practicing what I learned, Commander." The Ethiopian soldier stammered out in an attempt to keep a straight face.

"What? Are you an idiot?! In the Old City of Jerusalem?!"

My company had scheduled a week of training to take place in the forests outside of Jerusalem. My unit was being specially trained to be one of the first groups to enter the war zone in the event of a conflict in Lebanon and/or Syria. We had only been engaged in desert and hilly grassland training and needed to practice a few maneuvers in a forested environment. Captain Gasman, being ex-special forces, managed to get a hold of a few crates of paintball rifles for the training.

This week we had a little bit of an epidemic. It was a stomach virus characterized by diarrhea, vomiting, and fever. Only half of our group of seventy soldiers could go, and they made me stay on base. Of the forty or so soldiers confined to base, twenty of them were immediately sent home. I thought to myself that it wasn't so bad. I had been looking forward to the training but I really was ill. I knew I would deteriorate even more in the field. And I thought I could rest on base.

No such luck. They put me to work. At first it was just cleaning bathrooms and mopping floors. But then they made me pull weeds in the sun all day. I didn't mind working, but when I had a fever, vomiting, and diarrhea, it was just ridiculous, especially because no one else would help me work. They all claimed to be too sick to work, but it was painfully obvious that they were faking. We were all trying to see the military doctor because he was the only individual authorized to send people home. Our medic had to approve the appointment first. All the fakers had resorted to whining and causing the medic a lot of problems. Just out of spite he denied them all appointments. But I wasn't stupid. I figured out a long time ago that in situations like this a little sugar was often more effective than spice. I very politely talked to the medic and indicated that I was really sick, perhaps sicker than was actually true, and even commented in a patronizing tone that I felt bad for him because of everything he had to put up with. Out of twenty people the only two people who were granted an appointment with the doctor were me and another soldier who also wasn't whining like a three year-old kid.

We went to great lengths to make sure the doctor sent us home. First we ran laps around the doctor's office to increase our pulse. Then we filled up small glass bottles with hot water from a coffee machine and drank it right before they took our temperature. For me it didn't work very well. But for the other soldier it worked too well. He had to secretly pull the thermometer out before his temperature hit one hundred and thirteen degrees Fahrenheit (forty-five degrees Celsius) and cool it off a bit. He wanted to be sent home, not to the hospital.

For me I guess I didn't do it quite right and instead my temperature was slightly high but relatively normal. An orderly handed me a piece of paper with my temperature and told me to give it to the doctor. This was a big mistake, especially because the orderly used my pen to write everything down rather sloppily. Suddenly, somehow, my 37.0 Celsius (98.6 Fahrenheit) temperature miraculously rose to a 37.8 Celsius (100.3 Fahrenheit) fever.

In the end I got off the base, got out of weed pulling and floor mopping, and soon had a four day weekend. I would have rather done the training, but this was the next best option.

This week was simply a bad week to be in the army, especially because I noticed my condition worsening due to a lack of rest and being quarantined with other sick people. Forget that. I was going home.

And they called me a goody-good... I was not a goody-good. I just knew how to get away with everything, just like back in the United States. At that point the American police were probably still looking for me.

Once again I got into trouble for stealing chicken. I wasn't quite sure why this was becoming a recurring theme. I was working in the kitchen and they accidentally screwed me out of my lunch break so I hadn't eaten. There were absolutely delicious chicken strips coming off of a fryer/conveyer belt so I snatched a few. That was fine until the kitchen manager caught me and yelled at me for a few minutes in Hebrew. And he didn't like my excuse of not having eaten lunch. He didn't believe me

The following week I had been stationed in Hebron for another guarding assignment similar to my previous assignment just outside of Shechem. Two off-duty soldiers recently went hiking near their homes in Hebron. They were ambushed and killed by Palestinian Arab terrorists. My group of soldiers was stationed near there and we actually heard the exchange of gunfire. After that the more veteran soldiers in the IDF entered Hebron and began an intensive search. We heard quite a series of explosions.

When we returned to base there was a brief function for the *chayalim bodedim* (lone soldiers). It was a small speech complete with an impressive spread of refreshments and even free gifts for the soldiers serving in the IDF with no family in Israel, courtesy of Friends of the IDF. As usual I attended. When I arrived I was surprised to see WD-40 there. Although American by birth he lived with his family in a mansion near Tveria and therefore was not a suffering lone soldier in the slightest. Somehow with that slick tongue of his he had talked his way into the event, obviously motivated by the free food, gifts, and an excuse to get away from the commanders for a little while. I sat in the auditorium with my arms crossed, relatively annoyed at his deception.

The guest speaker called him to the stage to speak for a minute. The speaker asked WD-40 to explain why he had decided to become a lone soldier. All eyes were on him, including mine. I raised an eyebrow in anticipation, waiting to hear what kind of ridiculous cover story he could muster up at the spur of the moment.

Without even missing a beat he entered into a spiel about his dedication to the Jewish people and how much he missed his family. And then wiping a fake tear from his eye he choked up a bit.

"And without any family here it's like my friends in the Israel Defense Force are my family. Brothers, I would die for you!"

"Aw, that's so sweet," I heard a female voice say to the left of me. I glanced over and noticed for the first time that an attractive shooting instructor from San Francisco whom I had met a few months previously was sitting half a dozen seats away from me. She then addressed the male soldier sitting next to her in an almost accusatory tone, "Would *you* die for me?"

I rolled my eyes and sighed with unhidden irritation. Had WD-40 no shame?

Apparently not...

January 26th, 2008: Jumping Out of Perfectly Good Airplanes

The parachuting course was undeniably the most amazing experience of my life. The jumps were actually relatively dangerous because they were done at only four hundred meters (about thirteen hundred feet). That meant that if my parachute didn't open I only had about fifteen seconds to manually open my reserve chute before impact.

One of the instructors played a mean joke on me during training. We were engaged in a zip line exercise to practice opening the reserve chutes. Unbeknownst to me, they gave me a dummy reserve chute that was sewn shut and therefore didn't open. The idea was for me to slide down the zip line and when the instructor called over his bullhorn that my imaginary chute didn't open I would release my reserve chute and then land at the end of the zip line. As I slid down the line the instructor announced, "Chute failed to open," and I clutched the handle and gave it a good yank. It didn't open. I pulled harder. It still didn't open. This was just practice and there was no danger involved but still I was very engaged and screamed a long string of American profanity.

The instructors all thought it was hilarious. I actually did too after a few minutes.

After a week of training by jumping out of towers, dropping from zip lines, and various other activities we were supposedly ready. We climbed into the cargo plane and everyone was scared as hell. I had a psychological game I could play with myself. I called it "The Psycho Switch."[1] Somehow I just immersed myself into an insanely psychotic mindset and I felt like I could do anything. I genuinely just didn't care what happened to me.

In my psychotic state I stepped up to the door of the plane. Lunchbox commented later that he turned around to see an insane, glazed look in my eye. I walked up to the door whispering the lyrics of Drowning Pool's "Bodies." He said that if he didn't know better he would have assumed that I had been under the influence of illegal substances.

I stood at the doorway, watching the world pass by below me. Cool air rushed

[1 This was the origin of my nickname "Killswitch." The title was later modified from "Psycho Switch" to "Killswitch" not long after my involvement in Operation: Cast Lead.]

past my face as I prepared to step off into the void, chanting away my personal theme song.

The instructor gave me the signal and out I went. It was like stepping into a tornado. I was standing in a stationary position traveling at a couple hundred miles an hour. I simply stepped out and suddenly found myself spinning in the turbulence not just from the oncoming air but also from the force of the propellers. Thus the air rushing against me was doubled. It was like a huge hand of air violently snatched me and threw me into nothingness. I didn't feel like I was falling. I was flying. Because we were jumping at such a low altitude the parachute opened automatically after about three to four seconds. It was like entering the eye of a hurricane. At first all of the turbulent air and noise from the airplane and propellers engulfed me. Now that all vanished and I was just floating beneath the parachute. And the jump put my body into an intense state of adrenaline rush and shock. For me it was the greatest experience of my life.

The night jumps were even better. This may be rather morbid but for me it was metaphoric of death. I requested to be the first soldier out so I was standing at the door for about five minutes or so before the drop. I saw the full moon over the Mediterranean Sea, the lights of various Israeli cities and Middle Eastern villages, and gently rolling hills and mountains framed against the starry backdrop. I even saw my kibbutz.

"Hey, look!" I commented to the guy behind me. "I can see my apartment from here!"

It was one of the most beautiful things I had ever seen in my life. But just like Death you really couldn't prepare. Everybody had a different reaction. Some people were collected, some people degenerated into chaos, some people were scared, some people were assured, but no one was really sure what would happen the moment they made that transition and stepped out into the unknown. Also I had no control of the situation. The instructor informed me when it was time and I just jumped. Then the darkness took me and consumed me in a moment of extreme violence. And then all was dark, quiet, and peaceful. I was also falling, not rising, as if descending into the very abyss itself.

A common question was "What happened if you reached the door of the airplane and you didn't jump?" That soon became obvious. They pushed me out. On one occasion they pushed me out and I was highly irritated. It wasn't because I was scared to jump. I always requested to be the first one out because I loved it. Lunchbox had taken an extra second to get his footing and we were running out of time because we only had a fifteen second window when the plane was passing over the landing zone. I paused briefly, knowing that with the differential of our body weights he would need an extra second to clear the plane before I could safely jump. But the instructors wanted me to hurry. And I guess in their mind "hurrying" meant pushing me out the door. I almost collided mid-air with Lunchbox's parachute.

"Killswitch!" I heard him screaming in English. "Get away from my parachute!"

I responded in kind with a collection of profanity that ridiculed his weight.

The Israelis on the ground saw it and even heard it. I've been told there is video of it on YouTube somewhere.

Thus we completed the course to become bonafide Paratroopers. Quite often an ignorant individual would innocently ask if "Paratroopers still jumped out of airplanes."

"No," I would usually reply in my typical, smart-Alec manner. "They just call us 'Paratroopers' because it sounds cool."

February 15th, 2008: War Week

We had just completed the dreaded "War Week." Simply stated "War Week" was a week of intense training that essentially finalized our advanced training. We participated in numerous exercises that simulated large-scale military maneuvers. Many of the exercises involved assaulting and taking hills, working in conjunction with tanks, and endless treks across the Golan Heights. It was a complex movement with all of the various soldiers in our company and platoons covering and advancing to different points. Lunchbox covered my advance. He had several military specialties but one of them in particular was the gunner of the .50 caliber machine gun. As the lead designated marksman for the platoon I would go in first and set up to the left slightly to take out the snipers, charge to a better position, take out more enemies, continue to charge, etc. We also had an automatic grenade launcher to soften up the "enemy" before we went in, and not to mention a few soldiers toting LAW's (Light Anti-Tank Weapons).[1] The best part of it all was that we used live ammunition. There was a nice collection of abandoned tanks, jeeps, half tracks, and other vehicles scattered across the landscape. Yes, we greatly enjoyed blowing them up. It was a prime example of "boys and our toys." The Israelis often utilized an expression that described the situation perfectly: *"Chaim b'saret."* Literally translated it meant that we were living in a movie. It was like Hollywood for sure.

However, similar to a real war when we had completed the training attack what followed after wasn't much fun at all. We had no choice but to walk for what seemed like an eternity with at least fifty pounds (twenty-three kilograms) on our back (usually more). We marched a minimum of ten miles a day. Worse yet, we only ate once a day if we were lucky. And that was usually our infamous C-Ration supplies of a few cans of tuna, Loof, corn, and pickles.

The worst part, however, was the cold. It was *cold* here! I remember when I went to the Jewish agency in Los Angeles to discuss immigrating and joining the IDF. They told me how nice it would be to live in warm, sunny Israel. *Liars!* It was so cold during this War Week that the first few days were canceled because some of the officers came down with hypothermia. Later when it was "warm" during the training we were sleeping outside on the ground with no sleeping

[1] The LAW (Light Anti-Tank Weapon) was essentially a disposable rocket launcher. It consisted of a bazooka-like tube with a single rocket inside. After the weapon was fired it could be kept and re-armed at the factory or simply tossed aside if the former option was impractical.]

bags or tents. We had nothing besides a thin wool blanket. When they woke us up at three in the morning after about three hours of sleep I found myself covered with a layer of ice.

We also participated in urban warfare training again. We practiced breaking and entering buildings using both blanks and paintball guns. Again, as lead designated marksman it was my job to kick the door in and go in first. Accordingly, my position had the highest casualty percentage in the IDF. I was beginning to wonder if I got the job because my officers loved me or hated me. But I wouldn't have had it any other way. I wasn't a reckless fool necessarily but if I was going to come to the other side of the planet to fight in a foreign army I was not about to sit in the back and watch.

At this point I was becoming concerned that I had walking pneumonia. After the next few weeks I was going to demand to see a doctor. I wouldn't do it before the completion of advanced training because this preparation was invaluable and it guaranteed my position in important missions in the future. So I would just have to deal with it for a little while.

Advanced training was over for the most part. Soon we would complete a ninety kilometer march, which was about fifty miles. Yes, we would complete the entire ninety kilometers all in one sitting with basic equipment on our backs and only have a handful of five minute breaks. It would take us about nineteen hours. This was called the *Masa Kumtah,* or Beret March. And once completed we would participate in a ceremony wherein we received our coveted and highly-respected red Paratrooper berets. Immediately thereafter we would be sent to the front line. Right now we were planning on being stationed in Mount Hermon guarding the border with Syria and Lebanon. If there would be another war like the Second War in Lebanon we had in the summer of 2006 we would be first or at least second wave. After being there for a few months we would then be sent to the border of the Gaza Strip. I wasn't sure how much the American media talked about what was going on in the Gaza Strip or how accurate the information was, but I could say it was becoming quite restless.

I was hoping to come back for a visit to the United States for a month or so in May. But I was still unsure of whether or not this would be possible. The problem was that we were planning a large-scale combat operation.[1] And as the lead designated marksman of the platoon I had been given a significant amount of training specifically for these missions. I was unsure exactly when or even if we would be doing all of this, so I would have to try to plan my trip around my limited knowledge of that.

[¹ Even back then we were hearing rumors about the basic planning behind Operation: Cast Lead. It had been drawn up and sitting on the table for a long time before it was actually implemented. Prime Minister Ehud Olmert didn't really have the nerve to carry it out, instead choosing rather to initiate a six month cease-fire with Hamas. As could be predicted, the cease-fire did little to help international relations. Hamas used the time to visibly train and build up its military might. And almost immediately Hamas once again began firing rockets into Israel and planting bombs on the border. Oftentimes Hamas would conduct their terror operations in the name of allied terrorist cells, thereby claiming that it wasn't them, and therefore that they had not technically broken the cease-fire. Later even this pseudo-restraint was abandoned, but the international community did nothing to criticize their actions.]

February 22nd, 2008: Masa Kumtah (The Beret March)

Fifty miles never seemed so long. We started our march at about four in the afternoon and ended at eleven the next morning. It was nineteen hours of almost non-stop walking. We only stopped for a five to ten minute break every two hours or so, and we weren't allowed to sit down. And it was *cold!* It was so cold that in the morning after walking all night I saw in the sunrise that I was covered in ice from the morning frost.

We also smuggled an impressive collection of snack foods for the march. Commander Unibrow brought an oversized bag of gummy worms. That was great until the gummy worms froze. Yes, the gummy worms actually froze! They were a little crunchy but not bad. I recommend to everyone to buy a small package of gummy worms and to put them in the freezer. Afterwards eat them in the middle of the night with the air conditioner blasting on its highest setting while walking on a treadmill. Then you, too, can experience what it's like to train with the elite Paratroopers of the Israel Defense Force.

Because it was so cold I was wearing a knit hat and a *"cham tzavar"* (a "neck warmer" that was basically a cylindrical tube of scarf material specifically worn over the neck and/or face.) And because my face and ears were covered I was able to sneak my MP3 player onto the march. Everyone else trudged along struggling. I strolled along, however, bobbing my head to the beat of Korn, Alice in Chains, Nine Inch Nails, Metallica, Disturbed, Godsmack, and all of my other favorite bands. I put my MP3 on an alphabetical shuffle. By the end of the march I was on the letter "T". I had to be careful, however. A few times I saw my officer look at me strangely as I sang and moved along to the music that no one else could hear.

At the end of the march we arrived in Jerusalem and marched through the city. It was an amazing experience. The police blocked the roads off and people exited their vehicles to cheer us on and take photos with their cell phones. There in the Jewish capital amidst cheering and honking horns I felt like I had the support of the entire Jewish people regardless of political affiliation or religious background.

Then later we had our *Tekes Kumtah*, or Beret Ceremony. Commander Unibrow gave me his personal beret, which was a huge honor and I was very appreciative. Now I no longer looked like a low-ranking "newbie" in the IDF with the boring olive green beret. I now wore the respected red beret of the Paratroopers. I was also officially done with training and had earned the full uniform, complete with red-brown boots (as opposed to the normal black boots of other units),

Paratrooper insignia, Paratrooper wings, combat pin, and most importantly of all, the red Paratrooper beret.

I was in so much pain after the march, however, that I could barely move. I was actually concerned that I had hurt myself in the march. I was worried that I may have had stress fractures in my feet and legs. My right foot was especially swollen and painful. And when I took my boots off my feet were bloody. I guess there was a price to pay for that respect. But in the end it was worth it. I was sure my body would soon heal, but the Paratrooper respect was permanent.

I also went into a state of semi-shock. I think it was a combination of a lack of sleep and a caffeine crash after one too many energy drinks. At one point I even began to ask one of the sergeants in English if the reason he was always so sour was because his mother abused him as a child. Fortunately for me he didn't fully understand English and Lunchbox rushed me out of the situation before I could translate my question into Hebrew.

I was spending the night at Lunchbox's apartment. We were hanging out at his place for a while and I met his girlfriend and his roommates. We were planning on going out for a night "out on the town." But by nine in the evening we had all passed out in our various beds and couches. I was sleeping on the couch in the living room. Nobody told me, however, that there was another roommate that I hadn't met yet who was coming home at roughly three in the morning. Someone apparently had closed the top latch that prevented people from entering the apartment even with a key.[1] This additional roommate realized that he couldn't get in with his key and attempted to break into his own apartment, particularly by reaching his arm through the doorway and opening the chain latch. I jumped out of the "bed" and hid around the kitchen corner and pulled my five-inch double-sided military knife out of my boot. (By coincidence we didn't take our rifles home with us this weekend.) I decided to call him out and use a little bit of a bluff.

"Tell me who you are before I put a bullet in your head!"

This absolutely terrified him, which was kind of the idea.

"Give me one good reason not to put a bullet in *your* head?!"

He then whipped out his loaded Glock 9mm handgun and I heard the unmistakable sounds of *–slide, click!–* which could only mean one thing: he had

[1] It was probably me, but to this day I refuse to admit it.]

94

just locked and loaded his firearm. Needless to say, it was becoming a really ugly scene.

"Who are you and why do you have a gun in my apartment?" The voice on the other side of the door demanded.

"I'm Lunchbox's friend from the army. Who are you?

"I'm the Reaper, Lunchbox's roommate!"

"I met his roommates! He doesn't have any more!"

"Yes, he does!"

"Prove it!"

And so the conversation went until the Reaper was able to sufficiently prove his identity as friend rather than foe and I opened the door. We put our weapons down and properly introduced ourselves.[1] Ironically enough, we had this entire conversation in English. That alone should have been enough to deter us from the high level of paranoia and suspicion we had arrived at.

I was very disappointed with Lunchbox, however. He slept through this whole ordeal and had absolutely no appreciation for the fact that I almost died to save the lives of him and his girlfriend. What an amazing friend I was!

Regardless, I had learned a very important lesson: Never bring a knife to a gunfight.

[1] I soon befriended the Reaper even though he almost killed me. We are very close friends to this day and even business associates.]

February 28th, 2008: Anti-Boredom Activities

We had just finished advanced training and my unit was immediately deployed on Mount Hermon overlooking the Syria/Lebanon border in the Golan Heights. But I personally participated in a program of several weeks of Hebrew classes first and then I would go.

Already boredom had become a routine part of my military service. I had made a list of things to do on guard duty. Guard duty was a very important part of the service of an Israeli soldier. I soon discovered, however, that even in the most important guard post I still inevitably found myself looking at the same hill, mountain, village, street, etc., for hours. And after doing this everyday for... um, ever... I eventually became bored out of my mind. Therefore I had come up with a handful of activities to keep myself occupied and to survive the boredom attack.

1. Ponder the meaning of life.

This was what I usually started with. I surprised myself at what fascinating philosophical ideas I could come up with when I stared at the same thing for four hours. However, I usually became very depressed when I "pondered the meaning of life." Every time I asked myself, "What is the meaning of life? What is the purpose of my existence?" I always seemed to answer, "Kosher steak, kosher beer, and beautiful kosher women." And all three of these things were something that I simply had little to no hope of finding in the Paratroopers. And that was just depressing. I was also by nature an extreme pessimist, and the military had only accentuated this feature. An optimist looked at the beer as half-full. A pessimist looked at the beer as half-empty. I looked at the half-filled beer and exclaimed, "Hey! Who drank my beer?! Oh well, by now it's warm and tastes lousy anyway."

2. Playing with the Koom Koom

I was very proud of this one. This was my personal invention. One long night on guard duty I was protecting the main gate and sitting in a small circular tower with a *Koom Koom* (*"Samovar"* in Yiddish) in it. A *Koom Koom* was an integral part of Israeli culture and society. *Koom Koom* was a Hebrew term for an electric kettle. After filling up this kettle-like device with water and setting it on its stand the water would heat up until it began to boil. The *Koom Koom* would then shut off and I now had hot water for tea, instant coffee, cup-of-soup, etc. As usual it was very cold, which was becoming a recurring theme of my military service.

Then I made a brilliant discovery. If I waited for the water to start boiling and opened the top of the *Koom Koom*/electric kettle just before it shut off, the water would boil indefinitely and produce an endless quantity of steam. And at three in the morning I turned a small guard tower into a private sauna. It was glorious. Even more glorious was that I left the tower like that for the soldiers who replaced me. Sauntering back to my sleeping quarters I heard them express their shock with Hebrew obscenities when they entered the tower.[1]

3. Finding ingenious ways of sleeping

Most guard duty was important, sometimes vitally so, but often it was absolutely pointless and an utter waste of time. In such situations there was always the temptation of finding ways of sleeping *without* getting caught. This was especially true when they assigned multiple soldiers to guard something that did not require the guarding skills of multiple soldiers. One particular instance would be when I was sent to guard a group of thoroughly locked and bolted ammunition bunkers inside a locked barbed wire compound inside a walled and guarded base inside an Israeli city without a single Arab in sight, and many miles away from any Palestinian Arab city or settlement. The officers demanded that at least three soldiers guard these bunkers at all times. And what great threat was there to these ammunition bunkers that required such a heavy guard crew? Exactly. Two soldiers were supposed to be on "patrol" around the bunkers while one watched the gate of this barbed wire compound. It wasn't long before someone actually smuggled beds (yes, beds) into one of the empty bunkers and the "patrolling" soldiers had a nice nap while the soldier at the gate kept watch. He wasn't guarding from terrorists. He was watching for the commanders.

There was a saying in Hebrew we utilized here in the IDF. I saw it written as graffiti on the wall of the guard post of this ammunition compound. Translated into English it would be something like this: "When I was a child, I slept well because I knew someone was guarding me. When I was older and in the army I didn't sleep very well because I was always guarding. And now that I am out of the army I don't sleep at all because I know who is guarding me."

[1 *Important Note!* If after creating a private sauna in a guard tower you begin to see the fuse box give off sparks, smell an unpleasant burning odor, and hear the noises of "Snap, Crackle, Pop" like a bowl of Rice Crispies (TM) because of too much moisture in the enclosed tower, immediately turn *off* the *Koom Koom*/electric kettle and open the windows.]

4. Annoying trucks as they entered the main gate

My Canadian friend and fellow designated marksman, Axl, had mastered this

technique. Usually the main gate consisted of a large electric-powered metal gate sliding from left to right along a track. This was the standard main gate here in Israel for most military bases and kibbutzim. Axl, however, had discovered how to manipulate the power switch in such a way as to stop the gate half-way in its track. It soon became great fun watching a huge truck be forced to stop, back up, go forward, back up, go forward, etc., trying to get through the little space Axl had made for him at the gate. It was especially fun to engage in this activity against the trucks of rival army units, such as Kfir or Golani. After all, they deserved it.

5. Go back to #1 and repeat

At this point in time I was usually getting bored again and went back to pondering the meaning of life. I therefore returned to dreaming of kosher steak, kosher beer, and beautiful kosher women and accordingly became depressed.

March 7th, 2008: Terror Attack

I had a little bit of excitement this weekend. I was at the wrong place at the wrong time and got caught up in the middle of a devastatingly tragic terrorist attack in Jerusalem: the attack on Merkaz HaRav.

I finished the three-week Hebrew course and they gave me a three day weekend off from the army. I left my Paratrooper base near Beer Sheva and hopped onto a bus to Jerusalem. Meanwhile, a female officer in charge of the lone soldiers (such as myself) informed me that we had to be at a certain place Sunday morning to sign up for a special Passover program sponsored by the generosity of Friends of the IDF. But then I received a phone call from Commander Unibrow. He called me to try to revoke my three day leave and send me immediately to the Syrian border. But there were two problems with that. First off my unit was located on Mount Hermon and there was apparently a significant layer of snow on the ground and therefore transportation problems, especially on the weekend. Secondly, I still had to sign up for the Passover program on Sunday, and therefore simply could not go all the way to the north because it would be virtually impossible to come all the way back.

My commander told me to sit tight and he would get back with me later. I had numerous errands to run in Jerusalem and I was just "doing my thing." Then my officers called me back and told me again to go to the north.

And so I replied, "Okay, but what about Sunday morning?"

"Um... well... we don't really know," they answered.

And I had learned thus far *never* to trust the army, especially when it was quite obvious that they didn't have a clue what they we're doing (which happened relatively frequently when it came to administrative affairs). We continued back and forth like this until I decided to call the female officer to try to find some way to sign up without actually being there in person. And she said, "I'll get back to you." Of course she never did.

It was now approximately nine-thirty in the evening in Jerusalem and I was still waiting for the officer girl to call me. Near the Central Bus Station there was a *yeshiva* (Jewish religious school). Actually, there were two of them. They were run by the same organization but consisted of two separate buildings about two hundred meters (two hundred and fifty yards) apart. I was walking along, coming back from the supermarket to one of the *yeshivot* (Jewish religious schools) where I had several friends studying. One of them was Toohey, an

---

Australian I had studied with in my kibbutz *ulpan* and who would later become my roommate. On the way I hopped off the bus and started walking by foot. Then the police began swarming the area and ambulance after ambulance almost ran me over. I knew something happened but I didn't know what. I continued on to the *yeshiva*. When I arrived everyone was in a panic.

"The soldier is back with his gun! Quick! Help us lock the place down!"

"What happened?" I asked in shock as I locked and loaded my assault rifle.

In the neighboring *yeshiva*, Merkaz HaRav, a terrorist entered when the high-school aged Jewish students were having a pre-Purim party. The terrorist disguised himself as an Orthodox Jew and smuggled an AK-47 assault rifle into the *yeshiva* apparently in a box designed to transport Torah scrolls. He entered and sprayed the room with bullets, killing eight and wounding many others. An off-duty military officer[1] lived across the street and entered the *yeshiva* and killed the terrorist. He found him and emptied his thirty-round M4 5.56mm magazine into him. Meanwhile, as I was walking back to the other *yeshiva* we heard reports that there was another terrorist loose and the police started tearing the place apart for him.[1] The students of the other *yeshiva* were in a state of panic, fearing that their *yeshiva* would be the next logical target. I locked the whole place down, loaded my assault rifle, and knuckled-down into a defensive position to single-handedly guard the *yeshiva* against a terrorist maniac in a state of desperation.

I scanned the darkened street for terrorists with my loaded assault rifle, with sirens wailing, lights flashing, and police choppers hovering overhead. I had set up a barricade and kept my rifle pointed at the main and now locked entrance. Then an Israeli student waltzed up and asked me to unlock the door for him.

"There are reports that there is still a terrorist loose and this *yeshiva* is his next likely target." I countered.

"Yeah, I know," he replied. "But I really want to smoke a cigarette."

And out he went. He sat on the curb, smoking a cigarette with police choppers circling overhead, sirens wailing, ambulances arriving, and the Yasam police

[1] He was an officer in the Paratroopers and was soon promoted to major, I believe partly in recognition for entering the building and killing the terrorist. He later became my company-commander.]

force patrolling the streets[1] on motorbikes with submachine guns.[2] Perhaps that was the most disturbing thing about the attack. The Israelis were simply used to it. It was a pure tragedy when a culture had become absolutely desensitized to a terrorist shooting dozens of teenagers with an AK-47. Why were the Israelis so desensitized? Because unfortunately it happened so often.

After about an hour or so the police finally confirmed that there were no other terrorists and we were able to relax a little bit. But after five cigarettes and four cups of coffee there was no way I could sleep, especially because I usually didn't smoke. I guarded until two in the morning just to be safe until someone replaced me and I finally tried to get a few hours of sleep. After a restless night I got up at six in the morning to go to the Syrian border in the very north of the country like my commanders had ordered. At this point I couldn't have cared less about the Passover program. At eleven in the morning I finally arrived at the very north of Israel and found one of my sergeants, ironically the one whose attitude reflected a personal history of child abuse.

"Killswitch," he called to me in his usual sour demeanor. "They shut down the buses because of the snow so you can't get up the mountain. You can go home now."

I jumped right back on a bus and rode all the way back home and arrived at three in the afternoon, and therefore was sitting on several buses from six in the morning to three in the afternoon for absolutely no reason other than my officers' refusal to listen to me.

I staggered home to my apartment exhausted and in a state of semi-trauma. But I hardly felt to be in any position to complain, considering what the students and their families were going through.

[1 I later asked the major why the police thought there were two or possibly even three terrorists instead of just one. He replied that he deliberately lied to the police and told them that he thought he had seen another terrorist. He didn't trust the police and wanted to make sure that they properly secured the area and made sure that there were no other terrorists. It was a smart move.]

[2 The Yasam was notorious for being an absolutely brutal counter-terror police force. The funny thing was that they rode motorbikes and seated two cops on them. Initially I mocked the police operative sitting on the back of the bike because such a seating position was, in my opinion, an insult to his masculinity. But then I started watching them a little bit both in training and in action. Then I decided to keep my comments to myself.]

I was still waiting to hear the list of names of the dead/wounded to see if I knew any of them. I assumed that I did.[1]

Hamas declared the incident to be a great achievement, and pronounced a "national holiday" in honor of the terrorist attack. According to a poll conducted by Khalil Shikaki (a Palestinian Arab) and cited by both the Jerusalem Post and the New York Times over eighty-four percent of Palestinian Arabs supported the attack. I watched the news reports in which Palestinian Arabs in both Yehudah V' Shomron (the West Bank) and the Gaza Strip proudly, publicly, and joyously passed out candies in the street in celebration.

[1 I didn't know anyone who died in the attack personally but I knew several of them indirectly. You can still find photos and videos of the carnage on the internet if you do a search of "Merkaz HaRav" (or "Mercaz HaRav"). I didn't care how frustrated someone was politically there was absolutely *no* excuse for this. The average age of the dead and wounded persons was fifteen years old. There was no other government in the world that would be expected to tolerate this kind of indiscriminate bloodshed, especially of civilian minors.]

PART V: FIRST DEPLOYMENT
MOUNT HERMON
AND THE SYRIAN BORDER

March 26th, 2008: Snow Shoveling

For the past few weeks I had been located on the Lebanese-Syrian border on Mount Hermon. The elevation of the base was about seven thousand feet (well over two thousand meters). And there was actually still snow on ground. To my surprise somehow during the snowstorms the bunkers became filled with snow. The last thing I ever expected to do as a Paratrooper in the Israeli army was shovel snow out of the *inside* of a building.

Regarding my base I had become completely certain that the movie *Star Wars: The Empire Strikes Back* had been filmed there. The movie portrayed a Rebel base on the ice planet Hoth that was falling to pieces and incessantly freezing. That was definitely where I was stationed. Almost every day when I went to guard I expected to see the Syrians sending those giant four-legged Imperial Walkers through the snow to assault our base. Then Luke Skywalker would come speeding by in his slightly-less-than-science-fiction F-16 Falcon and take them out. And then I realized that I was way too bored on guard duty, and I went back to dreaming of kosher steak, kosher beer, and beautiful kosher women.

It wasn't long after I started my deployment on Mount Hermon and the Syrian border that I discovered that the IDF had made a slight mistake with my rifle. A few months ago we were switching out our rifles at the *neshkiah* (armory) because we were changing bases. As the lead designated marksman I was supposed to have a brand new M4 5.56mm assault rifle with a Trijicon day sight, specialized night vision scope, bi-pod, and counter-terror front hand-grip. When we made the transition from one base to the other I arrived a few weeks later because I did a Hebrew course. And in the meantime they issued me an inferior M16 short rifle that was probably one of the first ones made. The paint was chipping and it didn't even rack properly. They were supposedly temporarily out of the superior M4 rifles and just gave me that lousy M16 for a few weeks until the logistics people got themselves situated. But a few weeks later I reached the new base.

"Um, Killswitch," my commanders addressed me. "We made a little mistake with your gun."

"Okay," I replied, fearing the inevitable response. "What did you do?"

"Well, we accidentally gave it to the radio man/dispatcher."

"You what?"

Somehow my Paratrooper commanders gave the radio man/dispatcher, a soldier who just sat in a small room under the base a brand new, customized M4 assault rifle complete with several thousand dollars worth of scope packages. I had no idea how they made a mistake like that. "Dispatcher, lead designated marksman... Yeah, same thing." Thus the radio man now strutted around the base with his "cool rifle" while I did patrols and guarding assignments with a barely functioning cast-off. And to make it worse everyone routinely asked me, "Why on earth do you have that rifle?" The best part was when my own commanders asked me that, as if I had done something wrong. It got to the point that I didn't even bother answering. I simply glared back at them like they were the biggest idiots in the world.

I was recently making my way up north and was delayed, missing the last bus to my base. It wasn't a big deal. I simply stayed in a relatively small city in the north, Kiryat Shemoneh, at the *Beit HaChayal* [Soldier's Hostel] and took the first bus in the morning. Eventually I became bored and went exploring. I soon found a quaint wedding hall. Seeing that a wedding was about to start I went back to the hostel, changed into my relatively nice civilian *Shabbat* clothes, and invited myself to the wedding. Upon arrival I discovered that it was actually some kind of family reunion. It was one thing to crash a wedding, but to sneak into a family reunion was another accomplishment entirely. And to achieve this goal unnoticed with an assault rifle strapped to my back was simply legendary. There I was, drinking free beer, bumming cigarettes, eating free (and absolutely delicious) kosher food, dancing on the floor (with my rifle), and even getting photos with the family. They were such a nice family. I wonder who they were...

Not long after I almost shot an *ulpan* student/kibbutz volunteer. I had received a weekend leave and had returned to my kibbutz. I was clicking away on the computer in the *ulpan*/volunteer lounge, checking my e-mail and Facebook after spending several weeks on the Syrian border. Then I heard an extremely loud and strange noise. I never did completely determine what it was. Apparently, a moronic volunteer threw a bucket of water on some poor guy in a bathroom stall. In response the individual on the toilet took a chair and threw it at him, commenced yelling, and then started pounding on a hollow door in loud, rapid succession. To make it worse he caused the disturbance in the communal showers so the whole volunteer dormitories echoed with this staccato banging. My paranoia had already become quite well-known. And after being shot at twice in Hebron and being involved in the deplorable terrorist attack a few weeks previously I wasn't in the mode to mess around. In my defense at least two of the other volunteers panicked from the noise and likewise were concerned. I jumped up from the computer, let the profanity fly (hardly a big surprise for me), locked and loaded my assault rifle, and charged down the hallway of the dormitory with my 5.56mm carbine raised and ready to go. I came face to face with a Belgian *ulpanist* and utterly terrified him. I never did get a proper explanation.

"Dude, it's okay!" He repeated over and over again.

I was convinced that sooner or later someone was going to take away my machine gun.

April 28*th*, 2008: Course Commando Slave

I was given a brief vacation and I thoroughly enjoyed it. I went to a few weddings, drank, attended a few birthday parties, drank, hung out at the beach, drank, and, um, drank. Rocky-Roodle, the adorable British girl I had dated about a year previously also returned to Israel during that week. I was able to see her which was very nice. It actually gave me a great excuse to get out of the army. I talked to my officers and informed them that my cousin of the same first name was getting married, which was actually true. And my cousin was living in England for a while, which was also true. Then I suddenly changed stories and mentioned that Rocky-Roodle was coming here to Israel from England for a wedding, which was also true. Therefore the IDF assumed that it was the same girl (because they had the same first name) and gave me the week off to go to my cousin's wedding. I didn't lie to the army, and obviously it wasn't *my* fault that they got confused.

Afterwards my officers sent me to assist with something called "Course Commando." Essentially it was the Israeli version of Ranger school for the officers. It was an intense three-week course for various lieutenants to practice shooting, navigation, survival techniques, *krav maga* (Israeli hand-to-hand combat), and other advanced skills. I was given the "special assignment" of being their slave for three weeks. Most of the time I was working with two nineteen year-old female logistic officers who were not much more than little girls who had absolutely no clue what they were doing. All day long I loaded up trucks with equipment only to find out at the end of the day that it was all meaningless work because they had made a mistake. Then I would have to unload it all again. I was starting to get really annoyed. The best part was when they woke me up at three in the morning for a special task.

"Killswitch!" The little nineteen year-old blonde lieutenant yelled. "You need to get up right now!"

"Huh? What happened? Why?"

"We need you to work."

"What? Um, okay... And do what?"

"The officers doing the course are pulling an all-nighter and are hungry. Get up and make the forty guys all tuna sandwiches."

110

"What? Are you serious? You have got to be kidding me!"

"Hurry! Get up!"

Such was the glory and respect I was receiving in the Israeli Paratroopers. They actually pulled the lead designated marksman off of the front lines of the Syrian border to do this ridiculous assignment for three weeks. I couldn't believe it.

At first the petite blonde officer girl had a crush on me. And, of course, I did my best to take full advantage of the situation. In one case in particular we were located on the main Paratroopers Special Forces base near Netanya. She needed to check out supplies from the *neshkiah* (armory) and I tagged along. Because I was with her they let me in when they usually would not have. Obviously, because she was a *jobnik* officer girl she was goofing around and taking about half an hour to do five minutes worth of work. I was there right alongside of her, laughing, teasing, flirting... and stealing. There was a specific accessory to my rifle that I had been wanting for a long time. It was a forward hand grip but the Israeli military didn't like issuing them for some unknown reason. And I wasn't about to buy one. While I made the little officer girl giggle and blush I had my hands in the bins of rifle accessories.

Later, however, that little blonde lieutenant and I had a falling out during the Course Commando. I was assigned to a truck, loading it and unloading it senselessly. We were located in the field in the Galil about a quarter of a mile (half of a kilometer) from an Arab village. Then the truck broke down and we were stranded there all night. It wasn't a good scenario. It was just me, two unbelievably immature nineteen year-old female officers, and about a half-dozen soldiers that were all brand-new and most of them didn't even have their weapons with them. We set up guard rotations and shifts. But the Israeli military had a fear of trigger-happy soldiers. As a fully-trained Paratrooper I actually had a special card with my military ID that gave me permission to load my gun at all times on the front lines and at my discretion in all other circumstances. To me this was obviously a situation that warranted putting a loaded magazine into my assault rifle. But the next day after we survived the night the little blonde lieutenant saw my gun loaded and became enraged, claiming that I didn't have authorization. First of all I did have authorization. Unlike her I was a combat corporal and not a little girl sitting in a logistics shed. Secondly, even if I didn't have authorization I didn't really care. She could die if she wanted to. However, I preferred not to stroll around in the middle of the night next to an obviously broken-down military truck full of army equipment near an Arab village with an empty gun.

111

That was also the end of her little crush on me. Oh well. I guess it just wasn't meant to be.

I did learn something important during my slavery in Course Commando, however. I learned *"How to Change a Tire in the Israel Defense Force: A Ten Step Process."*

1. Realize that you have a flat tire, going through all the stages of grief: Denial, Depression, Anger, and ultimately Acceptance.
2. Determine who has the responsibility of actually changing the tire.
3. Smoke a cigarette.
4. Remove the spare tire from the truck.
5. Curse incessantly for at least five minutes upon realizing that the spare tire is flat, due to someone else having stolen your good tire and replacing it with their old one.
6. Smoke another cigarette.
7. Talk about the miseries of your love life.
8. Send one person out on a quick patrol to make sure no one is looking, and then steal the good tire from another truck.
9. Put on the new, good tire.
10. Put the old, punctured tire back in the spare tire rack of the other truck, ensuring that the other party involved will inevitably endure the same frustration you did at some undisclosed date in the future.

June 8ᵗʰ, 2008: A Month in the United States

After much prodding and begging I received my vacation to return to the United States for a month. Most of this sabbatical was funded by the amazing organization, Friends of the IDF. Friends of the IDF helps fund a program in which *chayalim bodedim,* or lone soldiers, are provided with plane tickets to take a month off of the military and visit their friends and family in their country of origin. Obviously I enjoyed myself immensely, but it was definitely a unique experience.

One of the strangest facets was that everyone spoke English. I had become so accustomed to speaking Hebrew that I was actually having problems conversing in English consistently. And apparently I had developed a little bit of an accent as well.

It was surreal coming back and seeing my old friends. I was particularly happy to see my best friend, DJ. We had been through a lot together. It was so nice to see that, despite the places that life had taken us, we were still such close friends. Although I had essentially been "camping" for the last year we embarked on our traditional camping trip, this time on the Navajo Reservation.

I also attended my Navajo ex-girlfriend's wedding. I was rather surprised that she repeatedly invited me to attend. The wedding was a traditional Native American ceremony on the Navajo reservation. I didn't think that the groom was particularly happy to see me, but I didn't particularly care, either. It was hard to believe that this had almost been my life, and how far in the opposite direction life had taken me. Watching the marriage ritual I had no doubt in my mind that I had made the right decision, as hard as it was at the time. And I finally had full closure of the ordeal.

Not long after I returned to Israel I received a new nickname. It was *"HaShadchan,"* or "The Matchmaker." I had a new hobby, if you will, of setting up my friends. One of these couples actually just got engaged. Thus *everyone* was now calling me and asking me to set them up. There was also a Jewish tradition that if a person made a match for three different couples he ensured himself a place in the World To Come. And considering the fact that I knew full-well that I was going straight to hell I figured it was worth a try.

I was reassigned in the Paratroopers, or rather, given a new specialty. I was still the lead designated marksman, but now I was in the *Mesayat. Mesayat* could best be described as the Heavy Weapons & Recon Company. It was the division of the Paratroopers that consisted of Humvee-based infantry specializing in heavy weapons, anti-tank tactics, and counter-terror ops.

The other night I was sleeping in a tent with too many soldiers in it. I was sleeping in a bed next to Axl, my Canadian friend sporting a close buzz cut. I was having a dream that I was painting a room and kept playing with the bristles and brushing my hand against them.

"Stop rubbing my head!" I awoke to Axl yelling at me in irritation.

Sure enough, there I was with my hand on his head rubbing away at his neatly trimmed buzz cut. I pulled my hand away in shock, and then burst out into laughter at the scene.

These past two weeks or so we had been engaged in some rather aggressive war maneuvers and training. We were specifically training at the bottom of the Golan Heights, simulating what would happen if either Syria conquered the Golan Heights in a war or if we invaded Syria. And with my specialty we were training with the Israeli *Shirion* (tanks), clearing out hills and wadis, from "Hezbollah terrorists" with anti-tank weapons. I was in the lead, bringing the troops up the hill, taking down the targets. Meanwhile, the artillery had just finished bombarding the area and the *retik* (heavy weapons squad) was nailing the hills with the MK-19 automatic grenade launchers and the .50 caliber machine guns. The tanks were in the back, slowly but surely proceeding and waiting for us to clear the area. The choppers were flying overhead to drop off and pick up troops as needed. It was simply awesome both to watch and participate in it all.

The terrain was difficult, though. It was nothing but rocks and thorn bushes. Running over rocks and diving into thorn bushes to avoid "enemy fire" wasn't a particularly pleasant experience. My legs were cut up and bloody by the time we were done, and I mildly twisted my ankle.

In three weeks I would have finished all of my training and be promoted to sergeant. From there I was going straight to the border of the Gaza Strip.

PART VI: MESAYAT
(HEAVY WEAPONS & RECON COMPANY)

July 25th, 2008: That Stupid Duck

We had been continuing war exercises in the Golan Heights, simulating an invasion by Syria. It was the same thing we had been doing all month. Attack this hill, clear out that valley, make way for the tanks and take out the "terrorists" with armor-piercing rockets.

In one of the exercises we scurried about a set of stone walls and ruins. At first I was concentrating so much on shooting, positioning, and flanking maneuvers that I didn't even realize where I was. Then I stopped to a look around and take notice that apparently we were practicing in some kind of ancient ruins.

"Where are we? What is this place?" I asked Sergeant Metalhead.

He informed me that it was some ancient city going back a few thousand years. The site was massive, consisting of at least a square mile (two square kilometers) full of trenches, roads, and five-foot stone walls. I asked why this wasn't preserved as an archaeological site or park. Sergeant Metalhead related that, while the place was undeniably interesting, it held no significant archaeological or historical value. Alternatively there was another site about ten miles away called Gamla that was similar and much more important.

"So... because it serves no real purpose, the IDF has decided to blow it up?" I questioned as I watched artillery cannons boom and tanks roll through.

"Yeah, basically," was my sergeant's reply.

At this time of year the Golan Heights was excruciatingly hot, which obviously made the training even more challenging. It also meant that the entire area was a fire hazard. In our combat vests we all held magazines of tracer rounds and our officers told us to make sure to remove them to avoid fires. We removed our tracer rounds that we rarely used anyway. Meanwhile, however, the artillery launched a heavy bombardment against their targets and the tanks were shelling it up. Likewise, the heavy weapons squad was annihilating the place with the automatic grenade launcher and .50 cal machine guns tore the scenery to pieces.

Accordingly, we accidentally set the Golan Heights on fire... Twice.

At first I thought we had thrown a few smoke grenades. But then it became apparent that it was an actual fire. We then called in the "Fire Crew," which consisted of five private-ranked soldiers running around flapping sticks with rubber mats at the end. I couldn't help but laugh.

We were engaged in chopper drop training in the Golan Heights. We waited for the Black Hawks to touch down, sprinted to the door, piled inside, and soared over the Kinneret (Sea of Galilee) to our destination. It was absolutely beautiful. It that moment I thought of Moshe Rabbeinu (Moses) and how he begged for the privilege of at least being able to view the Promised Land. And I understood why after gazing upon it he was finally content to pass on.

The problem with the chopper training was the landing. My chopper landed properly. But the pilot of the sister chopper (with Lunchbox inside) made a little mistake. The pilot was steering a landing on a large dirt patch in the Golan Heights but for some inexplicable reason there was a four foot (one and one-half meter) metal stake sticking out of the ground in the middle of this landing zone. The pilot landed the Black Hawk on top of the metal stake, impaling the helicopter. The metal stake actually spiked in between the legs of one of my fellow soldiers in the chopper, missing him by inches. The photos were unbelievable.

The Air Force, however, had a slight issue. They couldn't send out a crew to fix the downed chopper until the next morning. And my company somehow was "privileged" with the task of guarding the chopper all night.[1]

"Okay, listen up," our officers addressed us after we had completed our training exercises one day. "We need a volunteer to stay for the weekend and trade this weekend leave for the next one."

They weren't sure if they had the minimum six people to stay behind on base and they needed one possible volunteer. After about three hours of my fellow soldiers arguing and fighting amongst ourselves I finally said, "Enough." And I volunteered. But there was a problem because I needed to get out of the army on Sunday to go an engagement party for two of my best friends that I set up. I

[1] On the topic of helicopters back in the early to mid-90's several conspiracy theories were started that the American government created black super-choppers and President Clinton was on a rampage to clandestinely kill us all. I discovered where these mysterious black helicopters wound up in the end. They had been sold to the Israel Air Force. So if you ever see an ominous black

chopper floating in the sky there is no need to fear. It's just part of a Jewish army of Zionists. No conspiracies here!]
was supposed to have a three-day weekend and in the end I was fighting to get permission just to get off for Sunday for the engagement party. Friday morning I went to guard and someone was an hour late to replace me. There I was at guard duty and I watched the buses leave. When I returned to the barracks I saw that I was the seventh person there. They only needed six. In other words they just left me on base to close *Shabbat* and lose my three-day weekend for no reason. Usually such a thing only happened as a punishment. I was infuriated.

On Sunday I started begging my commanders again to let me out to go to the engagement party. I had been requesting the day off for over a month. They never told me I couldn't have the day off. My lieutenant simply never bothered to ask the superior officers for permission. Finally at noon I received permission to leave the base. But first I needed to get all of my equipment ready for some stupid inspection. I prepared my equipment, changed into my *aleph* (dress) uniform to leave the base, and asked my commander if I could leave.

"No," he responded with irritation. "I need to check your equipment. And what's your rush? There's time."

He was mad because he was in the middle of watching a movie and I was interrupting him.

"No! There's not time!" I retorted. "I have to be in Jerusalem in five hours and it takes at least four to five hours to get there from the Golan Heights."

After a continued argument the commander eventually did what he was supposed to and I finally got off the base.

I arrived in Jerusalem just in time for the party. I had previously set up my American-Jewish female friend with my Greek-Jewish male friend and they hit it off immediately. They held the party in a friend's beautiful home in the Old City of Jerusalem. And the future groom's rabbi from Greece also attended so I had the opportunity to chat with him. I always enjoyed talking to him because he was from the same area of Greece where my family originated.

Getting back to my military base the next day, however, was a different story.

Because I had unnecessarily lost my *Shabbat* leave I wasn't in a hurry to return to the army, especially when I knew that they weren't doing anything besides a pointless equipment check with the colonel. I slept in until eight in the morning, stopped by the military store to get some field supplies, had a nice brunch at a cafe in Jerusalem, and *then* I returned to the army. My officers had ordered me to "come back as soon as possible."

They had simply abandoned me on the base to lose my weekend leave for no reason and I was supposed to make sure I did everything in my power to catch all the right buses and run from one stop to the next to make it back to the Golan Heights? I didn't think so. I determined a way to buy myself approximately half a day. For one thing my officers had told me to return to my kibbutz from Jerusalem and to retrieve some equipment that I had left there and bring it to the inspection. Instead of doing that I simply stopped by the local Ricochet military surplus store and bought the same items for a nominal fee. Therefore I saved myself all morning. Also the local bus to the base from the nearest bus station in the north only ran once every three hours. When my officers called to find out where I was I told them I had just arrived to the bus station but had missed the bus by fifteen minutes so I would have to wait three hours until the next one. In reality I was still about two hours away from the bus station but it didn't really matter because I would make it with an hour to spare.

I had just gotten off the phone with my commander, quite content with myself for buying an extra half of a day off. Then I heard a female voice speaking in American English behind me. It became immediately apparent that she was a tourist that didn't speak one word of Hebrew. I discreetly took a peek behind me. There sat a cute, petite brunette and I saw my opportunity. She was a twenty year-old Jewish girl from Florida participating in a month-long Hebrew study program and volunteering for a few weeks on a military base. I commenced conversing with her in English and soon moved to the seat behind me and sat down next to her. After chatting away we arrived at a bus stop in the Galil in a city called Afula.

"You know," she said to me. "The local pet shop in the bus station here had baby ducks for sale a week ago and I really want one."

"Okay," I answered. "But you don't speak a word of Hebrew and the shopkeeper will rip you off and eat you alive."

"Yeah, you're right." Then she looked at me with big, brown Jewish eyes and said, "Will you buy the baby duck for me?"

I avoided laughing out loud and began to think about the situation. She was on her way to an army base for a volunteer program. I could just envision the looks on her *jobnik* (non-combat) officers' faces when this naïve little American girl innocently brought a baby duck with her back to the base. And I wanted her phone number.

Imagine the scenario:

There was a small pet shop in a small town in the Galil. A Zionist tumbleweed blew by. The shopkeeper lazily wiped off the counter. In strutted a Paratrooper in full dress uniform with a fully-automatic assault rifle in hand. There in the sunset stood a silhouette that inquired in a low, firm, quiet voice,

"You have ducks?"

"Yes."

"How much for a duck?"

"Fifteen shekels (about four dollars)"

The Paratrooper glanced to the left, then shifted his eyes to the right. And said with determination in his voice,

"Give me the duck."[1]

Yes, for all my efforts I did get the phone number in the end. But this was where the problems started.

Being distracted by the duck and the girl, I hopped aboard a bus going in the wrong direction and didn't realize it for about twenty minutes. I immediately

[1 He then tried to sell me two ducks, claiming that the first duck would be lonely without the second. I refused. The girl didn't need one baby duck, let alone two. The girl did take the duck with her to the military base where she was volunteering. The army commanders in charge of the volunteers were in shock and forced her to return it the next day. I wish I had seen the looks on their faces when this American girl showed up with a baby duck. All of my efforts, however, did little to impress her. I never dated her or even really talked to her again after that.]

123

jumped off the bus and switched directions. But then there was a freak car accident and what took me twenty minutes to ride one way took me over an hour and a half to return.

Now I had a problem because my commanders thought I was already at the bus station. I needed to get there immediately or else I was going to be in a lot of trouble. The only possible way to catch the five-thirty p.m. bus back to base was to take a taxi. But that would be quite expensive. Thus it became a question of how much I wanted to avoid getting in trouble in the army.

Staying out of trouble cost me two hundred and sixty shekels (about seventy five dollars) in taxi fare. And I barely made it.

That stupid duck.

The following *Shabbat* was worse. The lieutenant told me that I couldn't go home this weekend either because our unit was put on alert. He also informed me that I was assigned to be part of a bodyguard force for the colonel in charge of the entire Paratrooper Brigade on a different base. He agreed that it wasn't right and that it wasn't fair, but there was nothing we could do. As far as I was concerned I was ready just to let the colonel die but the IDF would have none of that and I soon found myself shipped off to a small base nearby to guard him.

This base maintained the worst living conditions I had ever seen in the army. To make matters worse, the persons in charge of the kitchen apparently declared that we were supposed to do all the work even though we were guarding. Accordingly, our commander led us in a strike and we told them to go pound sand. In return the kitchen told us we couldn't eat there unless we did all the work. After doing weeks of training with little food and sleep we were again faced with a no-food situation, this time during the weekend when we were supposed to be recovering. I went twenty-seven hours without food because of the strike. But our commander and a few of the soldiers sneaked off the base illegally to get themselves food. One of the soldiers coincidentally lived about three kilometers (two miles) from the base and his parents hosted them. I was guarding and starving to death and they were having a nice *Shabbat* lunch in a nearby village. Then the officer in charge figured out something was up and commenced a search of the base to find him and the other soldiers. Axl and I were doing everything we could to cover for them and fix a huge screw-up with the radios by ourselves. We then promoted ourselves for the day, seeing that our fearless commander had abandoned us and left us in charge of the emergency bodyguard force. The commander and his select crew of soldiers even had the audacity to go swimming in a nearby spring after lunch.

At about one in the morning after twenty-seven hours of no food the major heard about our strike, became highly irate, and ordered us to go to work in the kitchen. And by now there was no food left and ironically the soldiers sent to the kitchen were all those who had dutifully stayed on the base and accordingly not eaten. The soldiers who did eat just went to their usual guard shift. I felt myself crossing the line into pure rage. I felt myself ready to flip "The Psycho Switch."

The commander later apologized to Axl. He sort of apologized to me. But he wouldn't talk to me face to face. He actually called me on the phone because he had heard that I was ready to rip him apart. The Israeli commanders were just twenty year-old kids. They didn't like to admit it either, because they were insecure about their age. And in this case he was especially insecure as to the fact that a twenty-three year-old university-educated American was legitimately furious with him.[1]

We returned to our own base and there were even more problems. The officers told me that I had lost yet *another* weekend leave and probably also my two week vacation for various administrative reasons. Not long before that someone in my platoon refused to switch me out at guard duty and I guarded for two extra hours, which was absolutely unacceptable. It wasn't that an extra two hours of guard duty would kill a person, but it was the principle of the matter. It showed an extreme disrespect for their fellow soldiers and that they couldn't be trusted.

At this point I entered into a state of depression. It became painfully obvious in my mind that my officers didn't care about me, the commanders didn't care about me, and even my fellow soldiers didn't care about me. That didn't bother me. The problem was that we were in an army. If people were willing to leave me to guard for two hours extra because they were simply too selfish and lazy to change me out and simply didn't care, what would happen in a combat situation? When my officers routinely took away my leave and didn't make any effort to rectify the situation, what would happen when they sent me in first? If a person couldn't be bothered to get themselves out of bed to replace me on guard duty, then they would hardly be reliable when the bullets started flying and bombs started dropping. Combining this lack of support with the obvious incompetence

[1 This commander was later promoted and became an officer. By the time my army service ended he was already a combat lieutenant.]

of certain persons during our training exercise I literally began to lose it.
In the fourteen months that I had been in the IDF I had never become visibly
upset or depressed for any length of time. I ultimately developed the attitude
that I was in an American prison and needed to hospitalize someone in order to
get some respect.

By this time the officers began to realize that something was wrong. They kept
asking me but I told them I didn't want to talk about it. In the end I admitted
why I was upset. In fear that I was going to hurt somebody they sent me home
for two days. And G-d knows I needed the break.

I went home. But first I went to Jerusalem. Rocky-Roodle was back in Israel so
I met up with her and our other friends and we enjoyed ourselves immensely.
Finally getting my long-deserved weekend off and spending it with a beautiful
girl that I genuinely liked definitely raised my spirits and helped me get a hold of
myself.

The political situation with the Palestinian Arabs was worsening. For reasons
unbeknownst to me, the Israeli government had agreed to a cease-fire with
Hamas in the Gaza Strip. For a very brief while things had quieted down, but
now the terrorist activity was picking up again. I suspected that it was merely a
brief respite before the storm. And in a few weeks I was being sent to the front
lines of the Gaza Strip. And if there was a significant combat operation I would
be the first off the not-so-metaphorical Viking ship.

August 7th, 2008: The Gnome Garden

I finished the full training course and had been moved to the "Veteran Unit" inside the Paratroopers. At the end of all our training we had a ceremony. To my shock they called my name and gave me a very special award. It was called the *"Mofet."* Out of all the soldiers in our company I was declared to be the "Model" soldier of the year. In other words I was considered the most well behaved, the most respectful, and the best example of a good, loyal soldier. My response was a long string of hysterical, maniacal laughter. They just never caught me.

I received a special gold pin from the colonel commanding the entire Paratroopers Brigade. Everyone else was given a silver pin. Receiving the gold pin was a huge honor, although in reality it was essentially an award for being a kiss-up.

But it was then that I realized just how cheap the Israel Defense Force could be. The gold pin turned out to be just a silver pin coated with gold spray paint. It soon became chipped and looked terrible. If I ever saw this particular colonel again I was going to throw it at him.

In the battalion of 890 there were three sections: The *Palchod*, comprised of the riflemen and demolitions crew and was supposed to go in the front (but rarely did in actual combat situations for some unknown reason). The *Mevsayeet*, best known for their sniper platoons. And the *Mesayat*, which was the Heavy Weapons and Recon Company and where I had been assigned. We were the mobile infantry and specialized in various anti-tank and anti-personnel missiles as well as a groundbreaking new mortar system. On the base each company had their own "claim-to-fame", so to speak, at the entrance to the camp. The *Mevsayeet* emblazoned a panther painted on the wall. The *Palchod* proudly displayed a bloody spear painted on a large board. And what did we have in the *Mesayat* Heavy Weapons & Recon Company? A gnome garden.

Evidently somewhere in the Paratrooper ranks there was a logistics sergeant who was obsessed with these things. Correspondingly, he set up gnome gardens on various bases throughout the country. Thus when we moved from base to base we actually packed it up and took it with us.

When I used to envision myself in the Israel Defense Force back in the United

States the scene of transporting a gnome garden somehow managed to escape my fantasies.

When I was assigned to the *Mesayat* they placed me and my fellow soldiers in "Platoon 6." Each platoon had a nickname. I soon spied our title, the *"Barboniot."* It was a Hebrew word I wasn't familiar with.

"Mah zeh 'HaBarboniot'? (What are the *'Barboniot'*?)" I inquired of my new commander.

"They are," he answered in English with a heavy accent. "How do you say... You know, like the fish in 'Finding Nemo'."[1]

"The Clownfish?" I questioned, my eyes widening in disbelief.

"Yes, that's it."

"And why, may I ask, are we called 'The Clownfish'?"

"Because in the last war in Lebanon this platoon was known for being relatively stupid and wimpy."

"And so," I asked in horrified disbelief. "We used 'Finding Nemo' as the inspiration for our platoon nickname?"

"Exactly."

"You have got to be kidding me."

I had left the United States, joined the Israel Defense Force, passed try-outs to get into the elite and world-renown Paratroopers, finished over a year of training, made my way into the Heavy Weapons & Recon Company, and now I was part of the infamous "Clownfish"?!

Axl and I were very disturbed about this Clownfish business. So we took it upon ourselves to boost the morale of the platoon. For some strange reason my

[1 Apparently "Clownfish" was not the correct translation, and this was a mistake made by the Israelis. The correct translation would be a "Red Snapper," as if that was a significant improvement.]

officers had somehow gotten this idea into their heads that I was a master artist and painter. Every time they wanted a mural, sign, logo, or similar design to be painted they called me. I never really saw myself as the super-artistic type, but it was true that I did a better job than most other soldiers in the platoon. Maybe it was more a lack of competition due to laziness than an actual possession of talent. Regardless, Axl and I officially changed the platoon symbol and title to "The Fighting Hellfish" based on *The Simpsons* episode "Raging Abe Simpson and his Grumbling Grandson in 'The Curse of the Flying Hellfish'."[1] It was still stupid but at least it was better than the Clownfish.

Following the trend Axl and I were also asked to customize the Humvees with "6" logos and other related platoon designations. I took the opportunity to paint a Confederate flag near my usual seat of the military vehicle. As aforementioned I had initially utilized the Confederate flag in an effort to avoid confusion and corresponding "borrowing" of my equipment. But now the flag and symbol had begun to grow on me.

"Killswitch and Axl," our lieutenant addressed us. "This is your new sergeant and he will be part of this Hummer crew."

I had just finished painting the flag representing the Southern States and rose to meet the new sergeant. My face paled and I cursed under my breath to Axl.

He was an Ethiopian Jew with skin about as black as you could get. And he would now be riding in a Humvee proudly displaying the Confederate flag. Fortunately for me he didn't really understand what the flag meant.

"Is that the flag of Texas?" He asked eventually.

"Uh... Yeah, we'll go with that," I lied, taking advantage of his evident ignorance of the American Civil War. As our combat sergeant he consistently issued orders, bestowing upon us cleaning assignments and equipment

[1 In this episode of *The Simpsons,* Grandpa Simpson and Mr. Burns related the story of their military service in the fictional unit, "The Flying Hellfish." We used the Hellfish logo as the new symbol for the *Barboniot.* To this day the Israeli Military is still ignorantly endorsing the use of "The Fighting Hellfish" for unit t-shirts and to mark respective equipment. My apologies to Matt Groening, Jonathon Collier, Jeffrey Lynch, and the Fox network for any and all unintentional copywright violations. Please don't sue me.]

maintenance. And so a black African was bossing around a white American amidst displays of the Confederate flag both on the Hummer and on my personal equipment. Oh, the irony of it all...

Eventually, however, I came up with the most brilliant nickname for this Ethiopian sergeant ever. His first name was Baruch. Also the time frame was during the controversial elections with soon-to-be President Barack Obama. Thus whenever I felt that this sergeant was being a bit too demanding I would simply stand up straight and declare, "Yes, sir, platoon-commanding Sergeant Baruch Obama!" I usually got kicked for it but it was always worth it.

Right now we were having war between the ranks in the *Mesayat*. Somehow the non-commissioned sergeants had acquired way too much power and were fighting with the commissioned officers. The problem was that the sergeants were not always so intelligent. Even more so the higher the sergeant was, the less connected he was to actual combat. In effect they had become semi-*jobniks* and worked with logistics. It was a rude awakening that a not-so-smart logistic sergeant had more effective power than my commanding lieutenant that I went on missions with. The colonel himself was very upset about this situation and attempted to rectify it all. But there was still a little bit of a war between the ranks with commissioned and non-commissioned officers. And, of course, I was caught in the middle. Just to be obnoxious to each other they would intentionally give me orders canceling out the previous order I had received from someone else. I was getting three or four different orders in less than five minutes and I had no idea what to do. Then at least two officers would actually start yelling at me for "disobedience." This routine got really old, really fast. I had actually been standing in front of my lieutenant while he told me to do something and meanwhile the logistics sergeant stood behind him shaking his head and mouthing for me to do something different.

Finally I took a stand. Officially the commissioned officers, such as my lieutenant, were in charge. And the non-commissioned sergeants were simply out of control. I rebelled against the sergeants and only did what the commissioned officers said. The problem was that this action severely contradicted the "culture and tradition" of the *Mesayat*. It was safe to say, however, that I simply didn't care. In a few months we would be reinforced with a new draft of soldiers. And I would personally indoctrinate each and every one of them and make sure that they understood who to obey. If I had any say in the matter the dynasty of the *Sar-Sap* logistic sergeants would soon come to an end.

Recently I had been engaged in urban warfare training at a place called Tsa'alim. Tsa'alim was a massive mock village built in Israel by the American military for training. It was designed to replicate an Arab city, particularly in Iraq. Therefore I had dubbed it "Little Baghdad." It took about twenty minutes to walk from one corner of this huge training facility to the next. It consisted of buildings, streets, cars, light poles, mosques, and everything else imaginable. And the amazing thing was that it was all fake.

For two weeks we practiced taking over this city, shooting blanks and throwing concussion grenades. To make it more interesting soldiers from Givati, a rival unit, dressed up as Arab terrorists and were our "enemies." It was by far one of my most enjoyable training experiences.

During one of the main exercises the "referee," which was a major overseeing the exercise, decided that we had too many surviving soldiers on my side. He suddenly declared me and my Ethiopian sergeant, Sergeant Obama, to be dead. Apparently Sergeant Obama had stepped on an imaginary land mine and took me out with him. There we lay in the streets of Little Baghdad for two hours. But that was perfectly acceptable with me. I hadn't slept all night so I rather welcomed the chance to be dead for a while.

The most important aspect of this training was simply the reality of it all. My commanders made a few mistakes and we were ambushed once or twice. When we were in position but hadn't effectively cleared out the area and then a Givati "terrorist" shot a full clip of automatic blanks at us from ten feet away it really hammered it into our heads that we needed to pay attention and do the job right the first time. There were second chances in training but not in war.

Eventually we departed from our training base in the Golan Heights and were once again moving all of our equipment. Because we were the lowest ranking soldiers in the company we did most of the menial tasks. I felt more like a slave than a soldier. It was actually rather demeaning and depressing for a while.

Then the logistic sergeant started (once again) to annoy me. He gave me an order that directly violated our lieutenant's orders. We were supposed to have four people working for the logistic sergeant at a time. Then the fifth person was allowed to rest. The idea was for us to work for a few hours and rotate and have an hour break. The *sar-sap* (logistic sergeant), however, disagreed with this arrangement.

"No, *all* of you have to work."

131

"I'm sorry," I replied. "But that's not what we were ordered. The lieutenant said-
_"

"I don't care what the lieutenant said! He's not here. I am! And you do what I say! And you had better not mention the lieutenant again! Now get in there and organize my tent of equipment!"

That was a mistake. A big mistake.

To me the words "clean out and organize" would obviously include clearing out the trash and garbage. And in the *sar-sap's* private equipment tent I made a very important discovery: I found the gnome garden.

It was systematic. It was brutal. It was *garden gnome genocide*! I smashed every one of those stupid things and spread the remains all over the Golan Heights.

I wasn't present on the new base when they discovered the disappearance of the garden gnomes. I could almost see the look of heart-broken disappointment on the faces of these "hardened" warriors at the realization that they would see their precious gnomes no more.

Last weekend our commanders left me and Axl on a Paratrooper base near Netanya. We had about twelve to fifteen soldiers in our platoon. It was an abnormally small platoon and thereby we had problems. Each weekend that we were given permission to leave base we left at least two soldiers and a commander on base to guard, watch the equipment, help out with the kitchen work, and otherwise keep the base from falling apart. But my new commanders were relatively lazy and didn't want to stay the weekend. Thinking that my best friend and I were trustworthy they left us alone on the base with no guard duty, no kitchen duty, and no real responsibilities whatsoever. It was just me, Axl, free food, air conditioned rooms, and free satellite TV.

"Killswitch," one of my commanders addressed me. "Just don't sneak too much beer onto the base."

And so late Thursday afternoon the officers told us to have a good weekend and went home, confident of our responsibility and maturity.

That was another mistake. Another big mistake...

Israel was a very unique place because it was comprised of people from all over the world and from very special backgrounds. On my kibbutz, for example, I routinely ate lunch with a ninety year-old man who survived the Holocaust by outsmarting the Nazis and operating as a sort of double agent.. It was the same in the IDF with the new immigrant soldiers. And somehow we found each other. We all had our stories that we didn't tell and our backgrounds we didn't really talk about.

One such soldier was my best friend from Canada, commonly referred to as "Axl." Where the nickname came from I honestly never ascertained, because it wasn't original with me. But I had a suspicion that I didn't want to know. I knew it was a reference to his similarity to the nature of the lead singer of Guns 'N' Roses. He already had earned a degree in psychology from a prestigious university and spent his free time studying the lives of emperors and dictators, obviously planning to take over the world. I knew of his blood relationship to certain well-known and highly controversial figures, but for the sake of censorship I was asked not to disclose such information. There was even a rumor that he was a distant relative of Genghis Khan. I personally was highly skeptical of this rumor, but he did have slightly slanted eyes, which was a strange physical trait for a Jew to have.

Regardless, Axl was an amazing person. He was incredibly intelligent and unflinchingly loyal. If anyone was going to save my skin in the Gaza Strip I knew it would be Axl. And vice-versa.

After watching television and relaxing for a while we began to get bored. And what happened whenever Axl and I got bored? Nothing good.

The main highlight of the weekend was breaking into the colonel's office. First we tore through all of his drawers and cabinets, reading his files and trying to find something interesting to look at or confiscate. We didn't find much except for the speakers to his computer. So we took those. On the way out I found a picture of Moshe Katsav. Moshe Katsav was recently our president. Katsav, however, was impeached on the allegations of gross sexual misconduct. His picture had obviously been replaced with the current president, Shimon Peres. Purely as a joke I switched the photos and put the suspected rapist back on the wall. In about a month the colonel would be in a meeting and someone would notice it and exclaim, "Why on earth is that rapist's photo on your wall?!"

Later I attached my MP3 player to the speakers and started blasting Metallica throughout the base. Unfortunately, after about two hours I blew out the speakers. To me the only logical thing to do with the colonel's speakers after they ceased to function was to set them on fire.

We also found several grenades that could be fired from a M203 grenade launcher. But, not knowing what to do with them, we eventually put them back.

And it was then that we found another gnome garden! I couldn't believe it. But this one didn't particularly bother me. After all, if some logistics officer wanted his office to look stupid what did I care?

Rocky-Roodle, my British girl, returned to the country for a few months. We were spending as much time together as possible. We had actually been getting along much better this time around than the previous three times she visited Israel. We always got along fine, but for some reason it was even better than usual. We were having a great time together, seeing movies, going to the beach, spending *Shabbat* together, visiting the Old City in Jerusalem, and hanging out with our many mutual friends. I didn't know how long the good times would last, but I was making the most of them while I had them.

I was now immersed in a high-tech missile course. Israel had developed an innovative anti-tank and anti-personnel missile. In English it was called the SPIKE missile. I would continue this course for the next three to four weeks and learn all the details of the missile itself and how to operate it.

September 1st, 2008: Demoralized

My morale in the Israel Defense Force was dropping. I had been promised a promotion six months prior to the missile course, but I never got it. Although I was recently promoted to sergeant I was supposed to have my own squad and I was far away from that right now.

In the platoon we had something of a "civil war" and it had reached an unprecedented high. It was the *Olim Chadashim* Vs. the Israeli *Arsim*. The *olim chadashim* (new immigrants) were usually motivated. The Israeli *Arsim*[1] simply were not. The *Arsim* maintained a state of borderline rebellion, which meant that the Americans were forced to do most of the work. The commanders and officers were trying to rectify the situation. But in a mandatory draft environment when we were already very low on manpower there wasn't a lot they could do. If they sent someone to military jail for a few weeks, for example, then that meant the whole schedule would be negatively altered and the non-rebels (*olim chadashim*, in this case) would do more guard duty, more kitchen duty, more patrols, and receive less weekend leaves. Therefore it was a problem.

The *Arsim* ultimately gave the immigrants the collective name of "*Axlim.*" *Axlim* was a word developed on the basis of the Hebrew plural of Axl's name. The idea was that Axl was the leader of a band of obedient clones. I found this term particularly offensive because Axl was my partner in crime and not my superior.

Previously I had been dissatisfied with my partner squad machine gunner due to his distinctly weak demeanor, which was a very poor trait for the lead squad machine gunner. Eventually he was moved to a different platoon. Now I had a different problem. I didn't have a partner at all. We had three squad machine gunners in our platoon. But they were all Israeli *Arsim* participating in rebellion and refusing to take the machine gun. They whined that it was too heavy. We were engaged in counter-terror ops in the Israel Defense Force and we had soldiers complaining that a machine gun designed to rip a terrorist to shreds was

[1 *Arsim* were essentially the lower class of Israeli society. In the United States we had white trash and rednecks, and these were the Israeli version. They sported haircuts and clothes that would have sparked ridicule in the 80's. They wore "Aviator" style sunglasses and maintained an obsession with techno music and BMW sport cars. For more information go to YouTube and search "The Israeli Arse."]

"too heavy"?!

In the end the rebellion reached such a ridiculous level that they had to get Shaft, one of the Americans from Rhode Island, to become the new machine gunner. So now this American was the heavy machine gunner, the squad machine gunner, *and* the M203 grenadier all at the same time! He also had received no real training with the medium squad machine gun. And he was my new partner.

My question now became, "Who would be a better partner machine gunner: a coward, a wimp, a novice, or nobody at all?"

I came from the other side of the planet to help the Jewish people in Israel. I didn't come here to slave in the kitchen, clean the toilets, and volunteer to lose my weekend leave so they could go home instead. I *wanted* to be here, but I didn't *need* to be here. Simply stated I was tired of my dedication being abused. I was a volunteer and a soldier, not a slave or a pushover. It wasn't training anymore. We were not just goofing around on the Syrian border like we were six months ago. This was the Gaza Strip. This was about as close to a war as we were going to get.

I thought about the fact that I turned down multiple opportunities and requests to start a career in American intelligence or something similar with the amazing salary associated with it. I began to wonder if making my choice according to my ideals and principles was really worth it in the end. I had wanted to do something for the Jewish people. But at this point in my service what I was actually doing wasn't exactly what I had in mind.

The problem was that I was planning to have a career in the military or something related to Israeli national security. If I didn't receive my promised promotion then my chances of getting a good job were significantly decreased. When I had received an award from the colonel and had taken a peek at my computerized profile displaying the phrase "maximum recommendation for officer courses" and I still didn't get the promised promotions it was just depressing. If I messed up and failed, fine. I learned from it and did better next time. But when I did everything right and still failed, it was much more difficult to accept.

The officers were unsure of what to do. They understood completely why I was upset. They had expected the *Arsim* to break down and rebel. They hadn't expected me to break down and enter a state of extreme dissatisfaction. They were in shock. They couldn't believe that Killswitch, the ever-suffering, ever-striving super-soldier, had finally started to lose it.

PART VII: SECOND DEPLOYMENT

OUTSIDE THE GAZA STRIP

September 15th, 2008: Permission to Fire

We were now stationed on the outskirts of the Gaza Strip. We had an average of two emergencies per day. Whenever there was an emergency or alert, usually a Palestinian Arab attempting to sneak across the border and enter Israel, they sent my platoon in Hummers to hunt him down. My job as lead designated marksman was to sit in a high seat in the Humvee and scan the area with my day and night vision scopes and find him.

For the first time in all of my military service I *finally* felt like a true soldier. And the Israeli *Arsim* who just wanted to sleep all day and refuse to go on missions could go pound sand.

Last night we caught the perpetrator even. Or rather, Lunchbox and his platoon caught him. We were a convoy of two Hummers and an armored jeep. And the armored jeep captured him. I heard about it on the Israeli news the next day. Hearing about myself on the news would definitely take some getting used to.

So things were doing better from the standpoint of personal morale. The platoon still had some issues but at this point in time I didn't really care. I was doing what I wanted to do. I was using my training. I was finally beginning to have a purpose in the IDF.

The kibbutz had arranged for us to have adoptive families. And my "brother" was getting married. After many hours of begging and pleading with my lieutenant I got out to attend it. So I had twenty-four hours free from emergencies and alerts in the Gaza Strip. I had exactly one day to celebrate with my adoptive family and spend time with Rocky-Roodle, who was once again back in Israel for a visit.

Definitely one of the greatest blessings of my entire stay in Israel was my adoptive family on the kibbutz. The father was originally American, having made Aliyah shortly after the Six Day War of 1967. He was literally a genius, having a career in giving adult education.

The father was also one of the most inspirational people I had ever met. To summarize briefly he had been severely injured in the Yom Kippur War. How he survived was beyond me, honestly. He had been working to disarm mines. Unfortunately, however, he made a mistake. He lost both of his hands and most of his hearing. In spite of his serious physical handicaps he did everything in his power to make the most of life. Not only did he manage through his physical challenges he was an amazing husband and father. He had five sons and a daughter. Each one was unique in his/her own way, but they all shared the characteristics of being very loyal, very loving, and having a genuine sense of humor.

I will be forever grateful for all that this family did for me in that time. They went above and beyond the call of duty in showing me acceptance and hospitality. Not having had much of a family life myself I wasn't always the most amazing reciprocate in this relationship. But they really were an amazing family. I will always consider myself to have been greatly privileged to have spent time with them, especially the father.

Back on the line I was functioning as a short-range sniper in a pillbox overlooking a certain area in the Gaza Strip.

"Do you see the two males wearing black clothing about half a kilometer away from you?" Our military intel called us up on the radio. "They are a threat. Keep an eye on them and be ready to shoot."

I held them in the sights of my Trijicon scope, bullet in the chamber, safety off, waiting for permission to fire. Unfortunately, because of the supposed "cease fire", there wasn't a lot we could do unless they threatened us. They weren't stupid either, and only exposed themselves for a short while. So two terrorists lived to see another day.

I was very unhappy with the political situation. This "cease fire" literally meant "we ceased, they fired." The terrorists were violating the cease fire almost daily and we just sat around and did nothing. I was literally watching terrorists set up shooting ranges and blasting their AK-47's all day long, training to kill *me*. It was unbelievable. They would shoot their machine guns, look towards the Israeli fortifications on the border, and then continue shooting. It was insane. Oh, how I wished a war would break out. I didn't want a war, and I was not a stupid youngster craving action. Our analysts had said that if we entered the Gaza Strip right now and tore the place apart we would lose at least five hundred soldiers. But at the rate of training and rearmament if we waited until next year we would lose at least three thousand soldiers.[1]

Every day that we waited more people would die, both Israelis and Palestinian Arabs.

[1 In Operation: Cast Lead only ten IDF soldiers were killed, and that was mostly from friendly fire. The extremely low casualty rate of Operation: Cast Lead was a genuine and highly unexpected miracle.]

I was not a racist, and I was not even anti-Palestinian or anti-Arab. But these radical Moslem terrorists were a very serious problem. And they were as much, if not more, of a problem to the Palestinian Arabs than they were to us. All the terrorists wanted was destruction. If they couldn't destroy us they would destroy each other. Indeed, they had been destroying each other for decades.

I had never seen anything like it in my life. Even the Nazis weren't this psychotic. The Nazis wanted to kill, but they had plans and programs. With the terrorists it was simply a blind bloodlust.

September 25th, 2008: Cute American?

Although my attitude had gotten better I still had a few complaints. For one thing the *Arsim* liked to party outside my window for no apparent reason. They had the entire base to themselves. But for some inexplicable reason they felt compelled to hang out in front of my barracks room at two in the morning after I had come back from a mission without sleeping for several days. They actually refused to hang out in the air conditioned lounge, instead preferring to sit outside my window.

On multiple occasions I had gone out and very nicely asked them to hang out somewhere else. They declined, insisting that they would be quiet. That usually lasted about ten minutes.

Usually there was some *jobnik* girl with them. I despised *jobnik* girls. They were usually eighteen year-old little girls that knew that most of the soldiers drooled over them all day long. Therefore they felt that they could do whatever they wanted and likewise be as annoying as they wanted and most of the guys would put up with it.

But not me. Oh no… Not me.

Once again they were hanging out around my window. There was a *jobnik* girl visiting and the *Arsim* were frolicking over her. They were actually doing some kind of song and dance routine at three in the morning. All I wanted was to sleep for three or four measly hours. I stepped out and started yelling at them in Hebrew. I had already asked them politely several times to go somewhere else and they refused to listen. And the girl thought she could patronize me. Hearing my accent she said,

"Oh, what a cute American!"

"Do I look 'cute' to you?!" I screamed at her in a rage that could only be induced by several days of exhaustion from the field. "Get away from my window!"

The *jobnik* girls didn't try to flirt with me anymore after that. I wonder why…

A platoon was supposed to be comprised of twenty to twenty-five people. On a good day we had ten. This meant that, if we were lucky, we were doing double the work that we should have been. And it was starting to get to me. I was being assigned to work with the logistic sergeants more or less every day. This work involved toilet cleaning, sweeping, trash pickup, and other menial tasks. It wasn't a big deal if I did it, say, once a week according to a normal schedule. But when I did it almost every day it started to get really old. And the other guys were quite lazy and thus they refused to go to kitchen patrol. Accordingly, I usually ended up trading with them and went to kitchen patrol instead of working with the logistic sergeants. But I actually preferred the kitchen to the logistic sergeants. These sergeants were some of the most obnoxious people alive. And they did it on purpose. It was all just a show, like some kind of game according to military culture. But at that point I was almost twenty-four, a sergeant, and had finished basic training a long time ago and was getting tired of the immaturity of twenty year-old kids.

We also had a problem with the "veterans" in our company. The company was divided into two groups, the "youngsters" and the "veterans." The veterans had been in the IDF about a year longer than us and therefore claimed seniority. But it started to get out of hand. Some of them were even known for refusing to go on serious missions for no reason other than laziness. They thought they were hardened warriors. I thought that many of them were fat, lazy, and unworthy of the *k'vod* (glory/respect) that they demanded.

They also gloried in a long list of hazing rituals. Although the colonel had officially outlawed hazing it still went on. Axl and I didn't participate, however. Whenever they told us to make them coffee or pick them up on a chair and carry them around or something equally stupid we would simply make an obscene gesture and walk away.

What amazed me, however, was that the *Arsim* loved it. I couldn't believe it. They would often leave me stranded on guard duty or in the kitchen out of laziness but they wouldn't object in the slightest if someone from a different platoon demanded a cup of coffee. And they even began to criticize me for my refusal to participate.

"Killswitch, think about it," they tried to reason with me. "When we have the seniority then we'll get to do this to the new guys."

"Are you kidding me?" I sneered back at them in disbelief. "Do you really think that I get my kicks from demanding that newer soldiers make me coffee and other even more demeaning and humiliating tasks? Get a life."

The logistic sergeants especially were nasty in the spirit of this hazing mentality. Therefore whenever I was working for them I did everything in my power to make their lives and the lives of the veterans miserable. The sergeant recently told me to clean out the corridor between the disliked veteran's barracks and organize it. So I did.

"Killswitch! You call this organized?!"

"Um, yeah. What's the problem?"

"What do you think this is?" The logistic sergeant pointed at someone's makeshift ashtray constructed out of half of a Coca-Cola bottle.

"Well, I think it's an ashtray." I responded. "But being a soldier of my rank and position, I can't be too sure..."

"It's trash!"

"But I think someone is still using it..."

"I don't care!" He yelled at me. "I want you to throw it all away. Anything here that doesn't belong goes straight into the trash!"

Another big mistake.

So it all went into the dumpster. Running shoes, checker sets, unit flags, clothes, underwear, everything.

He should have been more specific.

Other activities included hiding chunks of raw meat in and outside the barracks of the veterans and logistic sergeants. After a day or two in the Middle Eastern sun the ensuing odor was atrocious.

On another occasion I was supposed to make a snack for a different platoon coming back from a mission. But the last time I came back from a mission they didn't bother to make me anything simply out of laziness so why should I have made them anything? I made it, as ordered. Then we finished making the snack and the logistic sergeant told me alone to guard it and make sure no one touched it until the soldiers came back from the mission.

Yet *another* big mistake.

Again, he should have been more specific. After all, no one told me *not* to crush up those jalapeno peppers and mix them in with the cottage cheese and other food items. And no one told *not* to dump out all the water so that they would have nothing to drink.

My personal favorite, however, was the incident in which I poured superglue into the lock of the logistic sergeant's personal equipment trailer. Axl later reported to me that he saw him take a sledgehammer to the lock, complaining about rust from the rain.

The logistic sergeants also had an obnoxious habit of playing *Mizrachi* (Eastern) style music incessantly. They had set up speakers on the roof and wired them back to a boombox in their barracks. I couldn't stand this music at all, especially not the same disc repeating constantly at three in the morning. I climbed onto the roof with a knife and gleefully sliced the wiring. Then I taped the wires back together with electrical tape without making a connection. The idea was that the speakers would then cease to function without it being obvious that the wires had been cut. It usually took them about a week to figure out that there was something wrong with the wire. Accordingly, they would rewire the entire speaker system. And accordingly I would climb onto the roof and cut the wires again.

One day I was strolling along the base and stopped dead in my tracks. The gnome garden was *back!*

As aforementioned I found another gnome garden on a different base. Somebody actually went to that base, picked up the gnomes, put them in the back of a pick-up truck, and drove them four hours down to our new base near the Gaza Strip. I couldn't believe it. On one occasion they had a special dinner for the veterans and they put the gnomes on the table. Regardless, their days were numbered. It was only a matter of time before they also came to an unfortunate demise.

To be initiated into the *Mesayat* Heavy Weapons & Recon we were required to complete another march. The march was only fifteen kilometers but it was actually much more difficult than I thought it would be. The pace we kept was very fast and we carried a heavy metal box of rocks the entire distance. Inside were the *Mesayat* insignias. I guess the mentality was that we were supposed to "earn" them.

The march really hit me hard, though, for some reason. I became severely dehydrated and my body went into shock. For some unknown reason my commanders didn't bother sending me to the medic upon our return. I didn't remember much, but I remembered at one point I started laughing hysterically, maniacally, and insanely for no apparent reason.[1]

"Killswitch? Are you alright?" My new lieutenant asked. "If I didn't know better I would say you were on drugs."

This made me laugh more.

"Have you ever seen him like this?" The lieutenant asked one of the other soldiers.

"No," he replied. "I mean, Killswitch is definitely quite strange, but this is beyond him even."

And that made me laugh even more.

It took me days to recover from that.

One of the soldiers in my platoon was an American born in Texas and brought to Israel at the age of five. His moniker soon became "Smirnoff," because of the resemblance of the name of the classic vodka to his last name.

Recently we were traveling from the Paratrooper headquarters back to our base outside the Gaza Strip on a chartered bus after completing a few days of refresher training. The commanders gave Smirnoff an award of going home a half day early. The moment he got off the bus he took off and made a dash to catch the next bus off of the base. He made no effort to ensure that his equipment made it to its proper location back on our base. Neither did anyone else. The bus drove off with his entire combat vest still sitting in the cargo hold beneath it. Unfortunately, the combat vest contained over one hundred and fifty rounds of designated marksman ammunition as well as a custom-designed night vision scope. But my personal favorite was the two live hand grenades. These items weren't exactly something we wanted to be sitting in a Lost & Found box at the local bus station. Lucky for him we got it back a few days later and kept it quiet. But I thought for sure he was going to be in a massive amount of trouble.

I made my way to Jerusalem the other day to fill out some paperwork for the military. I sat with Axl on a local bus near east Jerusalem and the Hebrew University. The bus came to a halt at one of the stops but was unable to proceed

[1 Immediately prior to the march I drank over a liter of Coca-Cola in an attempt to fight exhaustion. My body was rather sensitive to caffeine, and this fact probably had something to do with the shock, convulsing, and delirium that overtook me.]

because a van was blocking the entire road. The bus driver starting honking furiously but it still seemed like a long time before the van got out of the way. As we passed the van I noticed that the drivers were Arabs and that all the windows were covered. Instincts kicked in and I immediately jumped out of my seat (stepping on Axl in the process) and made my way to the back of the bus with my assault rifle ready in hand. The van then sped up and passed alongside us. Both the bus and the van stopped at a traffic light and the bus driver continued some kind of verbal argument with the Arab drivers. By this time I had returned to the front of the bus and continued watching them and gripped my gun. The Arabs didn't even seem to acknowledge the driver. Then they saw me. They pointed at me and sneered, laughed, and then pulled a U-turn.

Did I just stop a terrorist attack, or did I just almost shoot two civilians who had committed no crime other than a severe inability to drive?

About six hours later an Arab drove a Mercedes-Benz into fifteen soldiers about a mile or two (a few kilometers) away from where I had been. The driver had seen a group of artillery soldiers on a tour of the Old City of Jerusalem and decided to conduct a very simple terror attack. Was this all merely a coincidence? I would never know.

Back on the outskirts the Gaza Strip we occasionally conducted some missions. Most of the time when we were sent out we manned pillboxes (fortified towers) on the border. One of the mission assignments we were given recently was code named "The Song of Weeds." We were being sent into the Gaza Strip because the Palestinian Arab terrorists had a bad habit of placing explosives in the tall weeds next to the fence. They then would try to detonate the explosives as our patrols went by. The plan was to go in and pull the weeds while other forces covered us. I personally thought it was a pretty dumb plan.

In the end we didn't do this mission. Someone else did it instead. We were suited up and about to go when we got an emergency call to respond to two Palestinian Arabs climbing over the fence in a different location. They loaded us up and sent us with Jack the bomb-sniffing dog to try to capture them. The problem was that these terrorists crossed the fence in an area over thirty minutes away. And for some unknown reason they scrambled us to the scene instead of a closer unit.

So two terrorists got into Israel.

Recently intel reported that other terrorists had succeeded in placing three explosive devices along the fence. We sent in huge military bulldozers[1] to clear them out. But then intel followed up and told us that they had received a report that they were planning to try to blow up at least one of the bulldozers with RPG's (rocket propelled grenades).

Correspondingly, they sat me behind a concrete wall with a SPIKE missile launcher. My orders were that if the Palestinian Arabs fired even one bullet at the D9 bulldozers or anything or anyone else I was to launch a missile. My goal was to blow up a house we knew to be loaded with ammunition and explosives.

But the Palestinian Arabs evidently figured out we were ready for a counterstrike and thought better of it.

Once when I was sitting in the pillbox we were carrying out recon and spied two persons smuggling weapons into a wadi about five hundred meters away from us. We called it in to our intel. The intel confirmed the threat and gave us

[1 The bulldozers mentioned were the Caterpillar D9 Bulldozer. The military version was well over four meters (thirteen feet) tall and has been reported to have been able to withstand driving over six hundred kilograms (over 1,300 lbs) of explosives. In this case the D9 merely tipped over and the driver exited unharmed. This same D9 was the type of bulldozer that was involved in the death of Rachel Corrie, the American International Solidarity Movement activist killed in a controversial incident in 2003. In summary she tried to sit in front of this four meter, fifty thousand kilogram (thirteen foot, 110,000 lbs) bulldozer in order to stop it from demolishing a Palestinian Arab house covering a weapons-smuggling tunnel. It is still debated whether she was crushed intentionally by the driver using the D9 shovel/blade, or whether she was crushed accidentally by falling debris. It is also inconclusive whether she died at the scene, in the ambulance, or in the hospital. Eyewitness accounts varied dramatically, to the point that even the original accounts were painfully inconsistent with later claims. Either way, her actions were viewed as both illegal and irresponsible. The Israeli high courts rejected legal action against the driver, and the United States Supreme Court dismissed lawsuits against the Caterpillar Corporation. In an effort to show support for the Palestinian Arabs, Rachel Corrie's parents visited the Gaza Strip and the families she was associated with. In a moment of extreme misjudgment, however, a group of terrorists took them hostage. Hamas immediately rebuked the kidnappers and released them. Rachel Corrie's parents downplayed the incident to the media and the kidnappers mysteriously disappeared. The moral of this story is simple: Don't associate with terrorists in general, especially if that association encourages you to sit down and play chicken with heavy-duty military machinery.]

permission to kill them if they came any closer. Being the designated marksman on duty it was my task to take the shot if it came to it.

"They don't look like Arabs. They're Americans," my commander commented in Hebrew as we watched them from the tower.

"What?" I asked in surprise. "Are you sure?"

He then explained that he thought they were the Americans involved in International Solidarity Movement and other similar organizations. We had been having problems with them supporting Palestinian Arab armed cells and attempting to lure the IDF into situations involving violence and then presenting a deceptive report.

I sat in the fortified tower and watched through my scope half a dozen American "peace activists" with their arms full of machine guns and explosives. I really wanted to take the shot. I would have loved nothing more than to expose these fraudulent "peace activists" as the terrorist supporters that they really were. But they didn't come within range.

The other day our lieutenant, now dubbed Captain America[1], pulled me out of a mission. I was highly irritated. I asked him why he was pulling out his lead designated marksman. He informed me that it was because of kitchen duty schedules. I couldn't believe it. The soldier they replaced me with was not even a standard designated marksman. In fact, he had no specialty whatsoever and

was known for rebelling against the commanders. He even screwed over a sergeant by refusing to get up for his recon shift.

[1] "Captain America" was a nickname developed by Axl in reference to our platoon-commanding lieutenant. The title was derived from a character of the popular HBO mini-series, "Generation: Kill." Axl gave our lieutenant the nickname in a moment of frustration and I disagreed with him, considering the title harsh and undeserved. The officer in "Generation: Kill" was over-enthusiastic, bumbling, and incompetent. The nickname did stick, however, particularly because our lieutenant always maintained a high and perhaps unrealistic level of enthusiasm. I personally got along quite well with Captain America and to this day I consider myself privileged to have had him as my commanding lieutenant. Having said that, however, Axl and I will continue to affectionately make fun of him for the rest of our lives.]

It was in that moment that I realized that all of my hard work, my awards from the colonel, and my amazing profile didn't count for much. Captain America said that I was his most important soldier. I think he was just lying to patronize me.

October 1st, 2008: Smoke Signals

We received a new mission assignment. For security reasons I couldn't be too specific. To summarize briefly we did something in an attempt at fooling the Palestinian Arabs into believing that our defenses were down. We then clandestinely moved hidden kill teams into ambush positions. This lack of defenses would then provide a supposed opportunity for terrorist activity near the electronic fence. But, being prepared, we could monitor it and/or stop it.

The primary kill team consisted of six soldiers: A lieutenant, a sergeant/machine gunner, two snipers, and two designated marksmen.

I was the primary designated marksman. Axl was my partner designated marksman.

We set up an ambush position in a group of small trees and large bushes next to an oversized drainage pipe. At about three in the morning one of the commanders of *Palchod* called us up on the radio. *Palchod* was also part of the Paratrooper Battalion 890. They were a sister company to my company of *Mesayat* and essentially the Forward Rifleman company. Currently we were manning the pillboxes and conducting missions, especially ambushes, while they consisted of emergency response teams cruising the border in armored jeeps. There was a long history of rivalry between *Palchod* and *Mesayat*. The competition climaxed when *Mesayat* "attacked" the *Palchod* living area with a series of smoke grenades.[1]

"We are coming to your ambush site in our jeep to hang out there for a while and make sure all is safe," The *Palchod* commander called up Captain America.

"No," Captain America countered strongly. "We are hidden in a secret ambush. Do *not* come here or else you will disclose our position to the enemy. Carry on your patrol as usual."

"Okay. Well, we are coming anyway." The *Palchod* commander insisted, completely ignoring Captain America's order and clear logic.

"No, you are *not* coming here. We have set up this position in secret. What do

[1 The colonel of Battalion 890 was very unhappy with us for this action, and many soldiers went to military jail for a while.]

you not understand? If you come here you will give us away to the enemy."

"Understood. But we are coming anyway."

"Do *not* come here."

"We are on our way."

Axl looked at Captain America, shook his head, and sighed.

"I don't believe this," Captain America muttered. He immediately withdrew his military cell phone from his combat vest and called the company-commander of *Palchod* and demanded that he give his soldiers the order not to arrive at our location. Only then did the *Palchod* jeeps comply and keep moving.

That was the main problem with *Palchod*. They simply didn't listen and thought they ran the show. The army was like a team sport. If we played as a team, we won. If everyone did what he wanted and ignored what the coach insisted or what would help their fellow teammates to be as successful as possible, the team lost. It was that simple. But evidently *Palchod* hadn't figured that out yet.

They had made numerous grave errors lately as well. Recently a *Palchod* sniper was trying to take out a terrorist setting a bomb one hundred and fifty meters (about one hundred and seventy five yards) away. He missed. I never understood how or why. As a designated marksman with an M4 assault rifle even I could easily take out a moving target at that range, let alone a stationary target with a large-scoped sniper rifle.

The sun rose and we kept on the lookout. The usual time for terrorist activity on the fence was midday. They usually were not that active at night for various reasons. I had also been told that they were superstitious, fearing the imagined evil spirits of the night. Likewise, Israel traditionally conducted many of its operations at night even back in the days of the Hagannah before 1948.

We sat there in the drainage pipe the whole day watching. Honestly I didn't think the terrorists would be stupid enough to fall for our trick.

They did.

At about four in the afternoon I was sitting with Captain America and the sniper in the main observation area of our bushy hideout. The sniper was scanning the Gaza Strip across No Man's Land when suddenly two Palestinian Arabs came into his vision about fifty meters away from us.

"Whoa… Captain America, there are two males right next to the fence."

I grabbed my assault rifle and quickly checked to make sure that I was ready for action. I then crawled up a sand embankment and kept my head down. Meanwhile, Captain America quickly but quietly went to the drainage pipe where Axl had been sleeping and woke him up.

They were so close. Two males were walking along the fence with absolutely no clue that I was hiding behind them, gazing at them through the scope of my assault rifle. I was right on target. All I needed was permission to take the shot and I would have blown both of their heads off. There was no way I could miss at that range.

But in the Israel Defense Force we had a complicated set of Rules of Engagement, contrary to popular opinion and the portrayal of our military by the media. Basically I was not authorized to shoot anyone without special permission unless he was first of all visibly armed, touched the ground, and/or cut the electronic fence. If he was unarmed and tried to climb the fence I was not supposed to shoot him, or at least not kill him. However, if he was armed, then he was obviously a terrorist. If any part of his body besides his feet touched the ground then that also gave me permission to take him out. Palestinian Arabs had an irritating habit of setting land mines and other improvised explosives in the ground. Also, even if the Palestinian Arab dove to the ground before any exchange of fire commenced it showed first of all that he was staying for a fight rather than fleeing and secondly it dramatically reduced visibility to see concealed weapons. Thirdly, even in the situation that they were unarmed if they had wire cutters and started slicing the electronic chain link fence then we would kill them. A hole in an electronic chain link fence was not necessarily immediately apparent and it allowed terrorists to shoot through and throw explosives through the fence. It also held the possibility of damaging the electronic sensors, making it more difficult to detect other breaches. Additionally, when the electronic fence was cut the IDF had no choice but to send out civilian contractors to repair it. And Palestinian Arab snipers loved to target these contracted laborers.

I remained in my lowered position and watched their actions. Meanwhile, Axl joined me as Captain America called me down.

"Alright," Captain America explained. "Here's the plan. We're going to follow them secretly and from a distance using our *dilugim* (bounding) pattern."

I could always tell with Captain America if we were about to do something serious or just *stam* (unimportant and random). He didn't hide his excitement very well; the adrenaline got to him. His entire system sped up and he started talking fast. And he was talking *really* fast.

Axl and I nodded and we moved. Captain America moved first, sprinting from tree to bush to rock to concrete rubble, with me copying the pattern after him and Axl after me. It was in that moment I realized something. All that equipment became quite heavy. It wasn't easy to run with assault rifle, body armor, helmet, combat vest, one hundred and fifty rounds of 5.56mm ammunition, two liters of water, and more. I had always assumed that in a combat situation the adrenaline would make me forget all about the weight. Apparently not.

We followed them for about a kilometer. And then we realized where they were going. They arrived at a small, sandy hill overlooking our pillbox. The pillbox was on our side of the fence, and they stood on the hill on their side.

"Killswitch and Axl, get ready. Stay on target to take the shot if I command."

At this point they were about three hundred meters (four hundred yards) away. I readied my gun, kneeling behind a large concrete cube and resting the bi-pod of my rifle on the block. Looking through my scope I saw the two Palestinian Arabs holding something in their hands and point at the pillbox and obviously discuss it, planning something against the pillbox where I was usually stationed.

"Killswitch and Axl," Captain America whispered in his quick, adrenaline-hyped fashion, "We're going to take the shot. Be on target and shoot when I say."

I gripped my rifle a little bit tighter and held the glowing red dot of my scope on the upper chest of one of the targets. In seconds I would spend a burning piece of lead straight into his heart while Axl would do the same to the terrorist on the left.

Then the unthinkable happened. The unimaginable. The inconceivable.

Palchod arrived.

They had heard what was going down over the radio. Knowing that we had set up a perfect ambush they decided to show up anyway to steal the action and the glory.

Palchod raced up to the scene in an armored jeep and skidded to a halt facing the two terrorists. The terrorists, seeing the jeep, panicked. The first dove to the ground and the second got into a crouching position, giving us all the more reason to take the shot according to the Rules of Engagement.

"Okay," I thought to myself, "They are not moving too much so we can still take them down."

But then the stupidity of the *Palchod* bred more stupidity.

"Countdown to take the shot. 7... 4... 2... 1..." Captain America hissed.[1]

The commander of the jeep took his large mounted MAG 7.62mm machine gun and fired. But he didn't shoot at the terrorists even though he could have easily torn them to pieces. Instead he fired a bullet sixty degrees into the air, a warning shot.

Why did he fire a warning shot knowing that there was a secret ambush about to take the two terrorists out? Exactly.

"Fire!" My lieutenant yelled.

Axl and I fired. But the barrage of warning machine gun fire terrified the two terrorists and they both jumped backwards just as we pulled the triggers. I saw through my scope our bullets land exactly where they had been less than half a second before.

I cursed and kept on shooting as they made a hasty retreat. I saw my rounds land exactly between their legs. And the terrorists bounced from one leg to the next to avoid getting shot. If I hadn't been trying to kill them I might have thought that it was almost comical to watch. Then they dove onto the other side of a sand dune and started to crawl. We continued shooting, now at the small dust cloud rising as they scurried through the sand.

For a brief moment all was silent except for a strange ringing sound. Then I realized that it was because we were shooting 5.56mm assault rifles without hearing protection and now all I heard the bells ringing in my ears. Then after a few moments my hearing returned.

[1] In the Israel Defense Force when counting down for a salvo we said "7, 4, 2, 1, fire!" The numbers 3, 5, and 6 all rhyme with *Aish,* the Hebrew word for "Fire", and can cause confusion.]

BANG! – "*Expletive!*" – *Slam! ... BANG! -- "*Expletive*!" -- Slam!*

I looked briefly to the left to see what was going on. Apparently Smirnoff had recently borrowed Axl's designated marksman rifle for a bit of refresher training and put about a hundred rounds through it and "forgot" to clean it even though he claimed otherwise. Now at the worst possible time it was severely jamming on him. So severely, in fact, that the only way to load a bullet in the barrel was to slam the butt of the rifle on the ground while cocking it at the same time.

Meanwhile, *Palchod* and the armored jeep continued firing "warning shots" into the air.

"Killswitch!" Captain America ordered as I continued to pop off rounds. "Cease fire!"

"Why?!" I yelled back. "Just let me kill 'em!"

Reluctantly I stopped shooting and we watched and listened.

There was no movement.

Had we killed them? I didn't think so, but we did put a lot rounds into the small dust cloud. There was a good possibility that they had made the mistake of putting their heads in that small cloud. Then after what seemed like a long time one of them lifted their head at about four hundred meters away.

"There!" I shouted and we fired a few rounds. The head ducked back down immediately.

"Killswitch, we're going in!" Captain America called as he ran over to the fence, pulled out his own wire cutters, and started snipping away. Ironically in the heat of the action Captain America seemed to forget that Axl even existed at all and would give us orders collectively as "Killswitch".

Axl and I kept our scopes on the place where the terrorists had put their heads out while Captain America made it possible for us to enter. The lieutenant rushed through the opening with me and Axl following after. We were likewise joined by some of the officers connected to the colonel's force.

The eight of us did something that the battalion had not done ever since the cease fire with Hamas: we entered the Gaza Strip in a hostile situation.

We crossed half of No Man's Land, and the whole while I was watching the nearby village for snipers and terrorists with RPG's.

We ran the four hundred meters to the area where we had last seen the terrorists, with me covering the right flank. I expected the terrorists to have been long gone, or maybe to have found a body or two if we had been lucky with our shots.

To my shock we saw the two terrorists still on the ground... alive. We were told later that Axl and I had come so close to hitting them during the shooting so many times that they were afraid to move at all. And they especially didn't expect us to come in after them.

I was also surprised to see them up close. They were tall, but obviously young. Teenagers.

"Get up! Hands up! Get off the ground!" Captain America shouted at them in Hebrew. Being Palestinian Arabs, however, their Hebrew was rather limited. But with eight soldiers gripping assault rifles swarming around them I guess they got the message.

They were also extremely lucky that Axl's gun jammed so often. I was a crack shot. I was known for it. But Axl's marksmanship was legendary. It was one of the greatest mistakes of the IDF Paratroopers that he was never sent to the sniper course. He even won the competition for the best designated marksman in the entire Battalion.

The two young terrorists rose from the dust, one of them holding his own pair of wire cutters in his hand.

"Dude," Axl said to him in English while shaking his head. "You are *totally* screwed."

Meanwhile, I continued to cover the right flank.

"Captain America!" I called as he proceeded to search them for weapons. "They set off the smoke."

In Third-World Moslem countries "to sound the alarm" they ignited pre-arranged piles of debris and/or old tires. Thus I now knew that the entire Gaza Strip was about to explode and rain down on us, or rather, on *me*.

After quickly searching them for weapons and making them strip to their underwear we made them put their clothes back on and forcefully began to take them back to our side of the fence. The snipers told me later that they saw in the village the Palestinian Arab *ketat konenut,* or response squad as translated in English. Four terrorists pulled up to the outskirts of the village in a mule-drawn wagon, each carrying an AK-47. They were soon joined by three other men also with assault rifles. When I first heard about this response team I thought it was rather humorous. But later I realized that it was ingenious. The mule and wagon tactic was quiet, inconspicuous, reliable, cost-effective, and most importantly of all, not hazardous to the environment.

It was refreshing to know that the terrorists in the Gaza Strip were doing their part for the environment, too. For all their vices at least they were Green.

"Killswitch and Axl, cover us from behind! We're going back!" The lieutenant ordered.

Our eight man force began its retreat. It was then that I noticed that one of the officers from the other force was a Bedouin Arab recruited by the Israel Defense Force as a translator. Dragging one of the youths by the wrist he spoke rapidly in Arabic. I didn't speak Arabic at all but many of the words are similar to Hebrew words.

"So you thought you were going to kill some Jews today, huh?"

Then it all became Greek to me and he shoved the first teenager through the opening in the fence. He retreated to the pillbox and proceeded to bind him with cable ties and started the questioning.

"Killswitch! Let's go!" Captain America called to me, telling me to stop covering the rear and to retreat.

"Hey!" Axl called. "What about me?"

Again, our lieutenant had apparently forgotten about him and had given a collective order only to me.

I looked at Captain America dragging the other young terrorist through the hole in the fence. I then looked back across No Man's Land towards the nearby village and rising columns of smoke.

"Well, Axl," I shrugged. "You can do whatever you want. But I'm getting out of here!"

On their persons we discovered a large wad of cash and a cell phone. This cell phone had been given to them by Hamas. Their instructions were to walk along the fence to make sure that our defenses really were down and then cut a hole in the fence next to the pillbox. The moment they had finished this task they were to call the Hamas operative who would arrive to place explosive devices in the pillbox... *my* pillbox.

The two youthful would-be terrorists turned out to only be fifteen and sixteen years old. And when threatened with a minimum of five years in an Israeli prison designed for terrorists they started spilling everything they knew.

About that time the company-commander showed up. He was also the major who killed the terrorist at Merkaz HaRav and emptied his assault rifle magazine into him. He came over to me and Axl and congratulated us.

"But tell me," he admonished. "Why didn't you kill them?"

I just couldn't win. It was in that moment that I mentally gave him the nickname of Major Bloodlust.

I had found a jug of water in the pillbox and started passing it around. The Bedouin interrogator then asked me in Hebrew to let the two teenagers drink. I walked over to the prisoners and handed them the jug. I looked them in the eyes trying to read something. They stared right back at me. It was definitely an interesting experience, trying to kill someone and then treating him with courtesy less than five minutes later. All I saw was apathy masking an inherent hatred. I had just been trying to kill them. Indeed, the only reason they were still alive was because of a series of mistakes and coincidences. They showed no relief or gratitude that their heads were still on their shoulders. They honestly just didn't really seem to care.

There was no "proud defiance of the 'Zionist oppressor'." There was only a distinct air of disdain and extreme impudence. They knew what they were doing. And they knew it was wrong.

It was a difficult concept to grasp, that a sixteen year-old would have so little concern for his own life. I guess that was why they were willing to blow themselves up. They just didn't even care. The only thing they had in their lives was an intrinsic hatred for the Jewish people. I doubt they ever even questioned it.

Then one of the logistic sergeants who was also a driver showed up in an armored jeep to take our new prisoners away.

"Hey, Axl," I called to my friend as we sat in the pillbox tower. We were watching the hole we had cut in the fence to make sure no terrorists tried to enter and likewise to watch for any possible retaliation for our insertion. "The logistic sergeant is taking them. I guess he needs more workers. A few days cleaning toilets and working the kitchen and we'll get all the information we need."

And so that was the tale of my first two captured terrorists. They should have been dead, and I should have had two "X's" on my gun. But in the end it was better. The intel we got out of them was priceless. And I preferred to avoid shooting sixteen year-old kids. If I had killed them I wouldn't have lost any sleep over it. That was the way the war was over here. A sixteen year-old kid took a machine gun or an explosive and tried to kill people, and accordingly bet his life on the IDF soldier's sense of compassion. Placing that bet on me, however, was like playing Russian Roulette with a semi-automatic handgun instead of a revolver.

My mentality was simply this: "It shouldn't have to be like this. It really is a shame, tragic even…" *-BANG!-*

Later we went back to sitting in the bushes. We knew nothing was going to happen, but we went back anyway. It wasn't long before we heard the girl from dispatch comment on the arrest.

"Copy that. And way to go to *Palchod* for capturing those two terrorists. Good work."

Palchod?! That was the company who fired the warning shots and could have gotten everybody killed. And then it got even worse.

"Thanks, dispatch," I heard the voice of the *Palchod* sergeant who had blown our ambush respond over the radio. "I just want to say thank you to everyone for all their hard work. We did a good job today and lived up to our Battalion motto of 'We don't come back until victorious'. I also want to--"

At that point in time Captain America turned off the radio.

"I can't handle that guy…" he muttered and went back to sleep. It was his shift to rest and he wasn't about to waste it.

October 10th, 2008: False Alarm

A few days later our weekend leave was coming up. Immediately prior to going home Captain America told me to get my equipment ready. We were going out on a mission again. They sent me out in an armored Hummer with a mounted .50 caliber machine gun because intel had received another report that six terrorists were planning for something big at two in the morning.

Instead of sending out a handful of quiet kill squads half a day before they would allegedly strike they scrambled about a hundred soldiers an hour before the alleged attack at about one in the morning. And even if we had moved quickly and quietly it was simply not possible to hide over a hundred soldiers.

The terrorists never showed, which was hardly a surprise to me. I knew exactly what happened. I could almost see those terrorists and their reaction...

"Alright, guys. Are we ready to do this?" The leader of the terrorists asked. The other five terrorists nodded nervously and checked their weapons.

"Okay, let's take one last look to make sure everything is clear," The leader said as he grabbed a pair of binoculars and did his best to see shapes and movement in the darkness.

"What the... ?" The leader exclaimed. "There are over a hundred soldiers running around over there!"

Each terrorist looked at each other uneasily, not wanting to be the first to chicken out. Then one of them said,

"Hand me the binoculars... Wow, there are a lot of them. Forget this! I'm going back to bed."

The other five terrorists muttered in agreement and likewise went back home. And I spent yet another sleepless night staring across No Man's Land.

Rocky-Roodle returned to Israel for a visit, this time along with some of her family. I met her dad and brother while she was here. They stopped by for a two week visit. One evening her father informed us that he could get us into a traditional Jewish music concert for free and not pay the thirty dollars American per ticket.

But what he didn't tell us was how. It turned out that he had a hotel room with a balcony overlooking the concert. We pulled out some chairs and stole some cake leftover from a recent conference before the cleaning crew tossed it into the trash. We sat there in the warm evening air, listening to a concert in Jerusalem. He was definitely my kind of guy.

I had a few more days of my leave from the military. But there was a very real possibility that all hell would break loose in the Gaza Strip and my officers would call me back to base. According to our intel it was supposed to have happened twice already. And according to the media our politicians were openly admitting that we were planning a huge entry. It was just up to the IDF to decide how, when, and where. The problem was that if we did such an operation Hezbollah could cause us problems in the north just like in 2006. And even worse the new Russian military-issue Grad missiles that the Palestinian Arabs in the Gaza Strip had could now reach my home on the kibbutz.

Would there be yet another war in the Middle East? Survey said... Yes.[1]

[1] These entries were originally written months before Operation: Cast Lead was initiated. Even I was surprised later about how well I saw it coming, to the point of commenting on the missiles that would probably (and did) fall on my kibbutz.]

October 18th, 2008: Not Suicidal

It was the same story here. We were all sitting around waiting for a war. Morale was just getting worse and worse. It was so bad that they actually sent some kind of motivational speaker to try to counter the negative feelings. He basically tried to convince us that the reason we were completely inactive was because we had been doing such a good job that now there was a peaceful lull.

Yeah, right. As if we were going to believe that.

I said as much to him as well. The first lieutenant, Captain Crunch,[1] likewise tried to reiterate this idea. I told him to his face that I knew it wasn't true. We were sitting on the base and watching the Palestinian Arab terrorists rearm and train to kill us, not to mention enduring frequent mortar bombardments and watching Kassam rockets light up the sky. They were greatly enjoying the fact we had given them a chance to catch their breath and then they were going to hit us harder than ever.

I was very disappointed with the current policies of the Israeli government during the Olmert administration. The Israeli government was so concerned with what the world thought that they didn't want to do anything until the Palestinian Arabs broke the cease-fire enough to give us an excuse to counterattack. And even when they did repeatedly violate the cease-fire we did little to nothing in retaliation. But the world would never support Israel or the Jews. I thought we would have gotten used to this idea by now. And with Iran being given the freedom to spew out its verbal filth in the United Nations why did we care what people thought? I was the first to say that I did not support any ideas of genocide or even careless and reckless military actions that caused significant damage to civilian life and property. But a terrorist was a terrorist, and civilian casualties were an unfortunate and tragic fact of war. I wanted nothing more than to be unleashed to destroy Hamas.

Morale was at a critical level because our government had effectively told us that we had to sit on our hands and wait for them to kill us. And the moment that I and/or my friends started dying, *then* we could go in and do our job... maybe. But by then they would have rearmed and prepared and I and/or more of my friends would die.

[1 Captain Crunch received his nickname because he was very "By-the-Book" and even looked relatively similar to the classic cereal character.]

Our officers were trying to keep us from realizing the sad truth. But we all knew it. I looked Captain Crunch in the face and told him that I knew that all of this motivational stuff was ridiculous and insulting even. And he couldn't deny it.

The civil war between Hamas and Fatah continued. Hamas had just about taken control of everything in the Gaza Strip. It was unbelievable sometimes. The Palestinian Arabs slaughtered each other in the streets and alleys of their cities and villages. And apparently Hamas had a fetish with mortars. They simply launched mortars and cannons at nearby villages when they felt like it, both Israeli Jewish as well as Palestinian Arab population centers. Once I was sitting in an ambush and Hamas missed their target and sent a mortar off wildly. Unknown to them it landed a couple hundred meters away from me. My base was also within easy range of them. Recently I was placed in an ambush in an area that had been a forest until Hamas had extensively mortared it. Then it became little more than a wasteland of charred trees and holes. There were even a few unexploded mortars in the dirt.

On a different mission I was sitting in an ambush about twenty meters from the fence. Hamas had set an explosive device next to the electronic fence. This device was designed to be detonated by cell phone when one of our jeeps or APC's passed by. We found out later that we were sitting next to not just one bomb, but five. And one of them contained over one hundred and fifty kilograms (three hundred and thirty pounds) of explosive material. Because our intel had made a mistake I sat for two days next to over three hundred pounds of explosives.

I wrote a little note and left it in my personal belongings back on the base: "If I die here outside the Gaza Strip I want to make sure that everyone realizes it's because of sheer stupidity and not because of heroics or sacrifice and duty to my ideals, no matter what anyone tells you."

Speaking of my death my wonderful "friends" in the Paratroopers came up with a new prank. Somewhere along the line someone got this idea in his head that I was depressed. Well, obviously I wasn't exactly happy. No one here was. We were sitting around and waiting to get blown up. And I was personally annoyed with my officers because they never gave me my promised squad command and had essentially made a military career here in the Israel Defense Force either impossible or at the very least unrealistic. One of the *Arsim* of the platoon approached Axl and said to him,

"Hey, Killswitch seems really depressed. I think he might try to commit suicide. I think we should keep an eye on him."

"Are you serious?" Axl asked him in disbelief. He was my best friend and knew that the idea was ridiculous. If I ever became *that* depressed I think I would have just gone back to the United States.

"You want to keep an eye on him?" Axl asked. "Okay, then. You've got the first watch." He responded sarcastically.

I thought that was the end of it but apparently not. Somehow this rumor spread throughout the entire company and made it to the officers. Captain America and my sergeants likewise knew it was absurd. But Captain Crunch became very concerned. And the more I denied it the more everyone around me thought I was lying.

So my good ol' "friends," Axl and Shaft, decided to take it to the next level. Axl started drawing cartoons of me hanging myself, shooting myself, and otherwise violently killing myself and hung them all over the entire base and signed my name to them. Meanwhile, Shaft came to Captain Crunch and told him, "Hey, be careful. Killswitch has been talking about suicide all day."

I was put on unofficial suicide alert for about a week. Thanks, guys. With "friends" like these I didn't know why I was worried about terrorists.

Captain Crunch tried to "cheer me up" by giving me his special sniper gun maintenance kit. Meanwhile, Axl went to the commanders to request a new gun strap because his was broken. They told him just to jerry-rig it and make do. Thus I received a special kit and he couldn't even get basic equipment. I guess it was karma.

Axl legitimately was going into depression though. He had a lot of problems at home, particularly with his terminally ill grandfather. Additionally, his parents realized how dangerous it was where we were and it was just putting a lot of stress on everyone in his family. It was understandably hard to deal with. No one else really knew what was going on with him. When he became upset or depressed he just shut down and the Israelis, a people who didn't really hide their emotions, therefore assumed that everything was fine and dandy. Well, it wasn't.

I was doing my best to help him out even though there wasn't much I could do. Like I always said, if there was one person who had my back covered it was Axl, and vice-versa. If he left I was going to have some serious problems.

According to our intel the Palestinian Arabs had entered into a state of paranoia about our information-gathering techniques. They were so paranoid (legitimately) that they had come to believe some of the strangest things. My personal favorite involved the local stray dogs. In the Gaza Strip there were numerous stray dogs that somehow managed to make it through the fence by digging under or otherwise squeezing through spaces too small for humans. They then ran around our side of the fence for a while and eventually went home. The Palestinian Arabs apparently had come to the conclusion that we captured these dogs and hid surveillance and listening devices on them or even in them. They became afraid that the dogs were listening to them and giving us information.

Recently I was on an ambush and intel called us. They told us that two women were approaching the electronic fence and to be advised. Captain America understandably didn't want us to give away our position to counter two women unless we were sure that they posed a threat. We moved out of our ambush position to prepare to strike if needed. Then suddenly two donkeys came out of nowhere and half charged us, hee-hawing in full, angry force. Evidently they were "wild" donkeys and had been named by the intel personnel as "Bob and Margaret" after the British comedy. Once upon a time they belonged to a Palestinian Arab family. But now they were on the other side of the fence and couldn't get back. They now had an entire donkey clan running rampant along the fence, complete with offspring. I could almost hear the donkeys' conversation:

"Oh no, Bob!" Margaret the donkey exclaimed. "Look at this! We went to take a small vacation in Israel and visit our relatives, The Mules, and now they put up a fence! How are we supposed to go back to our owners?"

There was a brief moment of silence, then Bob responded, "Oh well, who cares? I never liked them anyway."

As aforementioned the terrorists had an extremely annoying habit of setting land mines and other explosives next to the fence especially amidst vegetation to blow up our jeeps and armored personnel carriers. I was waiting for the day when Bob or Margaret started munching on the wrong bush...

"Mmmm," Bob nibbled away contentedly. "This weed sure is tasty! What the...?"

-BOOM!-

In about a week or so two of my best friends were getting married. It was a particularly important occasion because I was the *Shadchan*, or Matchmaker. In other words I was the one who set them up. They wanted me to say one of the blessings of the *chupah* (wedding canopy) at the wedding which was a huge honor And in the near future the hard rock band, Slipknot, was coming to Israel.[2] I was trying to manipulate my weekend leaves to accommodate both of these events.

[2 They canceled the show and I never got my two hundred and fifty shekels (about sixty dollars American) back.]

November 9th, 2008: Special Forces Assault

Here in the Israeli army we had some kind of obsession with stealing equipment.[1] Much of this equipment was justifiably acquired for coming reserve duty after our three year minimum requirement of active duty. During reserve duty we were usually given inferior equipment so it wasn't a bad idea to sneak some of the better stuff home for later use. And everybody liked souvenirs. But some people apparently went a little too far with this "collecting." Every so often the IDF hosted a day in which citizens could return "acquired" military equipment with no fear of repercussions. Recently the military hosted one of these days. These were some of the more noteworthy items returned:

26	M16's
68	AK-47's
2	7.62mm MAG Belgian mounted machine guns
1	.50 caliber mounted machine gun
24	Night vision scopes and viewers
1	Part of a helicopter
33	land mines
690,000	5.56mm bullets

These were all items that people had in their basements or attics for no apparent reason. I always wondered who actually had land mines in their basement. Although I had to admit that land mines might have come in handy for a few ex-girlfriends that didn't get the hint to just leave me alone.

My personal favorite was the individual who tried to smuggle his entire *Merkava* tank home (similar to the M1A1 Abrams). He succeeded in getting eighteen pieces back to his residence.

I was very proud of myself the other day. I single-handedly put the entire base on emergency alert. I was guarding at the *Shin-Gimel* (main gate). Every day a small group of contracted workers came in to do various work activities such as construction, working with the antennas, or other manual labor tasks. I recognized the workers because they came to the base almost daily. Just out of

[1 When I finished my active duty I also fell into the trend and smuggled the following items back to my apartment: helmet, combat vest, two gas masks, flak jacket, sniper screen, half a dozen uniforms, extra boots, and much more.]

protocol I checked their ID cards and tried to call the dispatcher to verify that they had permission to enter. The radio wasn't working at the time so I let them in because I knew this was a normal routine. A few minutes later I heard the alarm go off and heard "Emergency Response to the Main Gate!" I stopped and look around...

Birds chirping... Trees softly swaying with the wind... Dog stretching out in the sun.

Then I realized something. The emergency response team at that moment was me and Axl. And we were also the ones guarding at and near the main gate. The other two soldiers apparently had "forgotten" that they were part of the team.

I laughed and shouted over to my friend, "Hey, Axl, the emergency response team is already here. It's us!"

By this time the officer in charge of the dispatcher had showed up and started yelling at me in Hebrew. He was upset that I had let the workers in without calling the dispatcher for permission.

"I tried to call," I replied. "But dispatch didn't answer me. And I checked their ID cards and followed all the necessary protocol. And they are the workers that come here *every* day. Do any of them not have permission to come in?"

"They have permission. But you didn't follow proper procedures to find that out. This isn't the end of this!"

He abruptly turned around and walked off as I gave him my middle finger behind his back. He later complained to our company-commander, Major Bloodlust, and demanded that I be put on a trial and be sentenced to a month of kitchen duty. Major Bloodlust told him to get a life.

Axl and I decided that it was obviously time to get back at the dispatch officer. We did everything to make the dispatchers' lives miserable when we guarded at the main gate. For example:

"Dispatch from Main Gate. Come in, Dispatch." I called over the radio.

"Continue, Main Gate."

"Copy, there is a very suspicious truck here requesting permission to enter."

"Who is it?"

"Checking... He says his name is T**** L***. Do you know the name?"

"No. What kind of truck is it? Is it military?"

"No. It's civilian. I think."

"What do you mean, 'You think'? What does it look like?"

"Well, it's kind of a big red van with the words 'Israel Postal Service' on the side."

"Are you serious? The mail truck? Let him in!"

And on another occasion:

"Dispatch from Main Gate. Come in, Dispatch." I called again over the radio.

"What now, Main Gate?"

"Copy. There is a very suspicious woman here at the gate driving a civilian vehicle."

"Who is it?"

"Checking... She claims that she's the major's wife."

"So let her in!"

"Dispatch from Main Gate. But how do we *really* know it's the major's wife? She could actually be part of an elaborate terrorist threat."

There were few things I enjoyed more in the IDF than finding ways to irritate obnoxious officers by doing exactly what they told me to do exactly the way they wanted me to do it.

The past month it had been raining relentlessly. In the Gaza Strip the ground consisted of very fine, dusty sand. When rainfall landed on this fine dust it turned to mud, and a lot of it.

This mud caused very serious problems inside the Gaza Strip. The terrorists were so blinded by their hatred for the "Zionists" that they ripped up the pipes out of the ground that constituted the sewage system. They then used these pipes as the casing to make homemade Kassam rockets to fire at Jewish towns. Meanwhile, however, areas of exposed sewage and waste lay scattered throughout the Hamas-dominated territory. As an obvious result local floods destroyed and contaminated everything.

The border crossings were usually shut down because of weapons smuggling. After the "disaster" various aid organizations significantly increased pressure on the Israeli government to let up on some of the restrictions and let more humanitarian supplies in. That seemed to be a somewhat reasonable request so we opened up the border crossings. Inside these "humanitarian supplies," however, we immediately found military supplies going to the Hamas terror cells.

Correspondingly, we shut down the border crossings again. The innocent person suffered and the whole world accused Israel of forcing the Palestinian Arabs to live in inhumane conditions. I wasn't really sure what the world wanted us to do. And we didn't tear up the pipes and destroy the sewage system in the first place. They did that in an attempt to *kill* us!

I honestly didn't understand why any person supporting the "Palestinian Arab cause" favored Hamas. To me it was the most absurd thing in the world. Hamas butchered their fellow Palestinian Arabs in the streets and villages. I watched hundreds of vultures circle the Gaza Strip every day. I had seen Hamas terrorists loading AK-47's in the back of cars and then drive off into the village. Minutes later I heard the machine gun fire and explosions, the body count of their political rivals steadily rising. And the world was telling us that if we killed anyone from Hamas then we were genocidal fascist murderers. I would have thought that the Palestinian Arab supporters would have been in favor of us getting rid of these terror-mafias that reigned with blood. Apparently not.

And every day I saw seventeen year-old boys climb over the fence without weapons. Many of them were trying to conduct terror missions but some of them simply wanted to get out of the Gaza Strip. They knew that they essentially had a choice of joining Hamas or rival terror organizations or they would be killed. Correspondingly, many of them instead attempted to jump the fence. They were fully aware that they would usually be apprehended and either sent back to the Gaza Strip or relocated somewhere in Yehudah V' Shomron (the West Bank.) But I couldn't say that I blamed them.

I especially found this fact interesting because the Palestinian Authority in Yehudah V' Shomron (the West Bank) had consistently complained about Israeli forces "occupying" the territory. I found it highly ironic how many Palestinian Arabs were trying to flee the Gaza Strip in order to place themselves under the "apartheid oppression" of the "Zionist conqueror." Maybe the "apartheid oppression" of the "Zionist conquerors" wasn't really "apartheid oppression" after all.

As previously related surrounding the Gaza Strip was an electronic fence. A mudslide disfigured about thirty meters of the fence. This damage was causing a huge problem and we maintained a constant watch to ensure that no terrorists crossed over. The Palestinian Arabs had previously placed a large number of explosives and land mines in the area. But the rain filled the wadi and washed all the mines back into the Gaza Strip, and now the Arabs were trying to get them back to the fence.

The imaginary cease-fire continued, in which the terrorists fired rockets into Israel and attacked our patrols almost daily and we did practically nothing in retaliation. But then we received an interesting order. Intel had related that Hamas had built a tunnel from one of their main military headquarters to enter Israel under the fence. The purpose was to kidnap more soldiers just like Gilad Shalit. We were given the order to prepare to destroy this tunnel.

The basic mission idea was this: Ten to fifteen soldiers from *Tzanchanim Palsar* (Paratrooper Special Forces, Counter-Terror Unit) were to enter the actual compound. Meanwhile, my unit of *Mesayat* (Heavy Weapons & Recon) was to follow with a tank unit and provide full support. Platoon Eight was to accompany the tanks to ensure that no RPG's were fired at the armor. Platoon Seven had the task of remaining on the edge of the fence, pinpointing heavy weapons threats, and mortar them. Platoon Six, my platoon, was the reactionary force. We were to go in with Major Bloodlust to wherever the most action was. We were also given the task of evacuating any and all wounded soldiers under fire.[1]

We started training for this mission. We particularly trained to enter burning

tanks and pull out the tank crews. Tank crews had lower physical requirements than the Paratroopers. This was a nice way of saying that I discovered that many of them were overweight. Therefore it took quite a bit of effort getting them out of the tank. And, of course, Axl and I were given the "privilege" of

[1 "My name is Forrest Gump. People call me..."]

crawling inside the burning tank while the others waited outside to help us as soon as we got them out.

The mission was all set and ready to go when the rain once again made a huge muddy mess. Therefore it was postponed.

Now it was a bright, sunny Friday morning. It was Halloween, ironically. The major commanding the battalion embarked on a patrol in his armored jeep with my friend, Afula, as his driver. They were responding to a recon report that two men were close to the fence. These two men, however, turned out to be terrorists with RPG's. They fired four RPG's. Two were fired at the jeep and two were fired at the nearby pillbox (fortified tower). One of the RPG's came within a meter of striking the jeep and blowing up the major and my friend, Afula. One missed entirely. The two RPG's fired at the pillbox destroyed it completely, but no one was inside.

It was the first huge, blatant violation of the cease-fire. Apparently placing explosives along the fence didn't violate the cease-fire. And apparently firing mortars and Kassam rockets at Israeli targets, both civilian and military, didn't violate the cease-fire. (I had yet to understand why, however.) But the RPG's were a little hard to ignore.

I spent the whole day watching the IDF scramble to do nothing. Even the air force came in and simply circled around for a while. We were under orders not to retaliate.

A woman came to the fence holding a bomb, a shovel, and a cell phone-based detonator. The captain of *Mevsayeet* (another company within Paratroopers 890 characterized by sniper platoons) ordered his soldiers in a jeep patrol not to shoot her, and to avoid even shooting warning shots into the air. The nineteen year-old female dispatcher actually told him over the radio to "be a man and do something about it." He finally agreed to shoot warning shots into the air.

Evening was nearing and I was stationed at an ambush point near the mudslide that knocked out thirty meters of fence. Intel called us and reported two men at the opening, most likely returning the land mines and explosives that had previously been washed down the wadi. Our commander rallied us up to go. We ran about a half a kilometer (quarter of a mile) to respond. But just before we got there the *Palchod* from Paratroopers 202, a rival battalion, showed up. When we arrived the *Palchod* jeeps sat motionless on the bridge, doing nothing as the two men ran off.

"Hey, who are you guys?" They asked. "Paratroopers 890? We're 202. What are you doing here?"

"Well," I replied with irritation. "We just ran half a kilometer and were trying to kill or capture the two terrorists who were just here at the opening at the fence."

"Oh yeah, we saw the two males. We have no idea what they were doing. But they ran away when we showed up. Why? What did you want to do?"

I muttered under my breath and cursed at them in English, Hebrew, Russian, Spanish, French, and German and just walked away. I couldn't take it. I had come to the personal conclusion that *"Palchod"* was not a name of an army unit. It was a really a Hebrew slang term for "mentally handicapped."

About five days after all of these consistently ridiculous scenarios we *finally* received the go-ahead to carry out our operation against the tunnel and Hamas compound. But during the briefing Major Bloodlust made a strange comment that our orders had changed slightly. The special forces units had requested that we wait even further back. And Platoon Six (me) was supposed to wait on base to respond in either the Hummers or the *Achzeriot*.[1]

We were highly agitated but there wasn't much we could do about it. We were also told that the moment one mortar or Kassam fell on the base we would go in.

About ten in the evening Axl and I were sitting outside listening to the distant melody of war. The unmistakable sounds of helicopters, jets, and gunfire permeated the balmy night air. And then there was a massive explosion. We assumed it was our special forces demolishing the compound and corresponding tunnel. A few minutes later we heard a nearing booming.

"Shh, Axl, listen," I said. "They're mortars."

"Yeah, I think they are ours." He replied quietly. "We're mortaring them."

I listened for a minute. The sounds drew nearer.

[1] *Achzeriot* were Armored Personnel Carriers that, once upon a time, were Russian T-55 tanks. Now they had been chopped up, the turret removed, new weapons and technology installed, additional armor put on, and functioned as troop carriers. After all, this was the Jewish army. We had to make some use of all those captured Russian tanks from the Yom Kippur War of 1973. Otherwise that would have been wasteful.]

"No," I corrected. "I think they're mortaring *us*."

Sure enough about half a minute later the mortars began falling near the base. The alarm went off with the infamous code "Purple Rain."[1]

The entire base scurried to the shelter. Axl and I threw on our ceramic body armor, combat vests, and helmets. We snatched our rifles and ran, ready to jump on the Humvees or *Achzeriot* (APCs). But instead of responding to the attack we were ordered to the shelter. Reluctantly with the shells falling around us Axl and I ran to the shelter.

Upon arrival I immediately realized that there wasn't enough room for everybody. That was definitely poor planning, in my humble opinion. I looked outside the shelter and saw an eighteen year-old girl almost having a heart attack and unable to move from shock. Tears streamed down her face. There was no room for her. I exited the shelter, grabbed her, and literally drug her and shoved her into the shelter.

An interesting thought crossed my mind at this point. I didn't really know this girl, but I didn't particularly like her because she was kind of immature and stuck up (like *every* girl in the IDF). I wondered if she would be nicer to me after I gave her my place in the shelter. I doubted it. But at that point in time I didn't really care.

Thus Axl and I stood outside the shelter and watched the bombs fall. Then we got an idea. We went back into our rooms and turned on our poor substitute for a stereo. We then started playing ACDC's "Shook Me All Night Long" and the Mamas and the Papas' "California Dreamin'." I particularly related to the lyrics, "I'd be safe and warm if I was back in LA..."

Meanwhile, we were waiting for the order to go in, which was supposed to come at any moment.

To pass the time and to get into the spirit of things I decided to get into my Goth get-up. I figured if I was going to go into the Gaza Strip with guns blazing I was going in with style. With mortars falling and explosions shaking the windows I painted my nails black and put on black eyeliner and lip liner. If it scared the Palestinian Arabs half as much as it scared my fellow soldiers they would flee in

[1] Yes, we actually named our code for incoming mortars after an outdated Prince song. Only in the Israel Defense Force...]

177

horror from the sight of me.

The order to retaliate never came. We sat there all night, waited, and watched the mortars fall. One fell about one hundred meters away from me. I heard both the whistle as it fell and the deafening boom that followed.

I found out the next day what had happened. Apparently various generals and colonels commanding different special forces units all wanted to get in on the action. So instead of sending in the initial ten to fifteen counter-terror Paratrooper special forces as originally planned about two to three hundred special forces soldiers showed up. These special forces units included *Sheldag* (based on the British SAS), *Shayetet* (similar to the US Navy Seals), *Ya'alom* (demolitions special forces), *Orketz* (K-9 special forces), *Orev Tzanchanim* (special forces, anti-tank missiles, Paratroopers), *Palchan Tzanchanim* (special forces, demolitions, Paratroopers), and about three times the amount of *Palzar Tzanchanim* (special forces, counter-terror, Paratroopers) as originally planned.

All of these special forces soldiers showed up without a proper plan and completely decimated the original strategy. The counter-terror Paratroopers ultimately did enter the compound. Afraid that the structure was heavily rigged with explosives they sent in a robot first. Sure enough, it was booby-trapped. Hamas blew up the compound and their tunnel themselves.[1]

And then all hell broke loose. But because these various special forces units wanted all the action they demanded that the tanks and accompanying Paratroopers (i.e. me) wait outside the fence. Between the Palestinian Arab houses and the fence there was about a kilometer of No Man's Land. This kilometer was just emptiness, void of rocks, trees, or anything else. The tanks and our mortar squads sat outside the fence while hundreds of special forces soldiers milled about in No Man's Land without a proper plan.

The terrorists started firing mortars, but the special forces soldiers had nowhere to go for cover. Six of our soldiers were wounded from the mortar fire for no real reason.

At one point our mortar squads had pinpointed one of the main clusters of enemy mortar launchers. They were about to fire when an air force general called over the radio and said, "Under no circumstance will you fire on those Meanwhile, the soldiers who had been trained for this mission with the weapons

[1 I never determined what happened to the robot. I assumed nothing good.]

and equipment designed for the task sat impatiently back on the base. And in my case I was listening to classic rock 'n' roll and playing with my creepy cosmetics.

mortars." A few minutes later two F-15's swooped down and dropped their payload onto the enemy mortars and sent them straight to consummate their seventy-two virgins.

After this whole mess the Israeli government had stated that they wanted to maintain the "cease-fire," and that this was just an isolated incident against an isolated threat.

Hamas, however, didn't feel the same way. They claimed that because they hadn't actually used the tunnel yet they had not truly broken the cease-fire. I guess their mentality was that preparing to kidnap more Israeli soldiers during a time of "peace" and committing a war crime in direct violation of the Geneva Convention was completely acceptable as long as they hadn't actually done it yet. Only after it was too late and they had kidnapped a collection of soldiers like Gilad Shalit was it permissible to retaliate. But if the IDF carried out a select operation to stop this specific threat then *that* was a violation of the cease-fire. And somehow the whole RPG attack had been dismissed. Hamas had a habit of making arrangements with allied terrorist organizations and thereby claimed that they weren't "officially" responsible. They purported this mentality that terrorism by the same people under a slightly different name made a substantial difference. Because we supposedly broke the cease-fire Hamas now declared themselves free from any "obligations" of peace. Evidently they had forgotten about all the other RPG's and Kassams that they had been firing, as well as the numerous improvised explosive devices that routinely awaited Israeli patrols. Now the Kassam rockets and mortars continued to fall even more than before.

At this point I had grimly come to realize what I left my home in the United States, my friends, my good job, my cars, my girlfriend, and everything else, for. Any illusions that I was fighting terrorists, making a stand for Israel, and doing something honorable by supporting the Jewish people were all completely false. I felt that I was merely cannon fodder for terrorists. And I washed the dishes of the Israeli people and cleaned their toilets on occasion.

As ironic and unbelievable as this may sound, I was bored out of my mind.

After all this I finally was given my weekend leave. I went back to my kibbutz by way of Sderot and Ashkelon where most of the Kassam rockets had been falling. It was heartbreaking to look out on beautiful coastal Jewish towns and see column after column of smoke rising from apartment buildings, schools, and synagogues. Seeing it on television in my living room in the United States was sad. When I saw it in person it was far worse. When I had friends that lived there it was unimaginable. And when I felt that I was failing in my responsibility to protect the Jewish people from such attacks it was unbearable.

In the first two days after the special forces mission they fired over fifty rockets. Later it averaged about ten per day. When a rocket was fired our warning system gave local residents between five and seven seconds to get underground before impact.

The newest missiles that the Palestinian Arabs in the Gaza Strip claimed to have could hit my kibbutz.

Hezbollah boasted that their new missiles could hit any point in Israel north of Beer Sheva from Lebanon. Beer Sheva was the southernmost point of civilization before the long expanse of the Negev Desert. In other words Hezbollah in the north could hit not only Haifa and Tveria like in the war in 2006, they could now hit Tel Aviv, Jerusalem, and also my kibbutz if they were so inclined. There wasn't a single square inch of Israel with the possible exception of the southernmost tip of Eilat that was not under threat from terrorist rockets and missiles.

One of my best friends was a South African-Israeli commander nicknamed Weeman. Before he was drafted into the IDF he participated in a volunteer program in Sderot when a barrage of Kassam rockets fell on the city. He described seeing a young girl about fifty meters away from him have her legs blown off. He tried to help her but she bled to death.

Axl still wasn't doing well. His grandfather was dying here in Israel. It wasn't a good scene. The grandfather survived the Holocaust and so in his dementia he was back in Auschwitz. He thought that his son and grandson (Axl) were Nazis trying to kill him and screamed at them in Yiddish. Axl dealt with the army and went home and tried to help his father care for his grandfather. It was really hitting him hard psychologically and emotionally. Therefore it was hitting me hard as well. Axl and I made a pledge at the beginning of the army to stick together and watch each others' backs. After all, neither of us had a whole lot here. Even the fact that his father was here in the country was a recent development. And my family life had deteriorated years ago. It was frustrating because I had my own issues to take care of and there wasn't a lot I could do for him. I mean, what could I do? About the best I could do was listen to him when he needed it but that wasn't as easy as it sounded. Thank G-d he had an amazing girlfriend. But there were times when they talked on the phone and she admitted to me later that she just cried when he hung up.

Life in the military and facing the greatest depravity of mankind could take everything away from me. It could destroy my ability to love, to think rationally, and to believe in the Powers that be. But there was one thing that could never be taken away from me: alcohol.

I embarked on my weekend leave for four days with one goal in mind: to stay so drunk that when I returned to the Paratroopers on Monday morning I would have little to no memory of what I had done. I just wanted to forget, for a few sweet days just to forget it all.

I did my Goth thing and attended a metal concert in Tel Aviv. It was a good show. I moved with the crowd, screaming at the top of my lungs and nobody noticed or cared. I randomly bumped into a few friends of mine there and we went to a metal club after the concert. At about three in the morning I started trying to make my way back home. Sometimes I could find a *sherut* (taxi-shuttle) at late hours to take me the forty-five minutes ride back to my apartment on the kibbutz. This time, however, they apparently weren't running or I had just missed the last one. It was unfortunate but there was a bus at five in the morning and it was a significantly cheaper anyway. I was hanging out for about an hour and a half outside the central bus station in Tel Aviv. At four in the morning there were a handful of Russian gangs loitering near the bus station as well. I didn't particularly care. I didn't bother them and they didn't bother me.

But then I heard gunfire. I looked in through the glass doors of the bus station. Some Russian gangster had apparently taken a handgun and shot one of the security guards point-blank and taken off running. He burst through the glass doors and took off down the street with pistol in hand and half a dozen of security guards chasing after him. They popped rounds off from their 9mm pistols as they ran. To my knowledge he got away.

The one time I didn't have my assault rifle with me was when something like this happened. People made fun of me because I took it *everywhere*. People laughed at my paranoia.

I just stood there. There was no fear, no anger, no adrenaline, no excitement, no curiosity, no concern. There was simply no emotion.

I later thought about the Merkaz HaRav terrorist attack that I had been present at, where the Arab terrorist butchered fifteen year-old students with an AK-47. I remembered how shocked I was that the Israelis were so used to it and unexcited. They were angry, of course, but unexcited. And it was then that I realized that I had become one of them. Cold. Thoughtless. Emotionless. Brutal.

It was then that I also realized that I was already sober.

Once upon a time I believed that the power of life and death was in the hands of G-d alone. I had realized that this was simply not true. The keys of hell and death were in the hands of men. And the world would be much better off if men did not have this power.

They were the slaves of the Angel of Death. As I related these events in my journal I looked down and stared at my M4 assault rifle and scope sitting on its bi-pod and loaded with almost sixty rounds of sharpshooter ammunition.

Maybe I had become his slave, too.

November 29th, 2008: The Prime Minister Visits

A few weeks ago the prime minister of Israel, Ehud Olmert, came to our base to give us a speech in a hopeless attempt to encourage morale. Currently the prime minister's popularity rate here in Israel was practically non-existent. Nobody, right wing or left wing, liked him. He was seen as ultimately responsible for his miserable failings in the Second War with Hezbollah in 2006. He had also been caught in numerous laundering and other monetary scandals. In the Paratroopers especially his popularity was very low because he wanted to divide Jerusalem and give away half to the Arabs. But it was the Paratroopers that re-conquered Jerusalem back in 1967. We weren't particularly thrilled about the idea of giving it away for many obvious reasons.

Prime Minister Ehud Olmert was scheduled to arrive at our military installation that afternoon. Accordingly, that morning the Secret Service showed up to secure the area. The whole day Axl and I ridiculed them in English, knowing full well that most of them understood us. They were so poser, complete with CIA-style sunglasses and ear pieces. They were obviously trying to copy American movies.

Then I noticed a crew of Secret Service agents checking the Coca-Cola vending machine to ensure that no one had placed any explosives inside. And it was then that I realized the irony of it all. The Secret Service in their diligent efforts to guarantee the safety of the highly-unpopular prime minister had failed to realize that he was coming to visit a military base with hundreds of soldiers. And they had failed to notice that each of these soldiers possessed an assault rifle and at least two hand grenades on them at all times, not to mention having practically unrestricted access to rocket launchers. But at least the prime minister could rest assured that there were no bombs in the soda machine.

One of our Paratroopers did insult him, though. He asked Prime Minister Ehud Olmert how he could praise us and encourage us to be willing to die for the State of Israel when he wanted to just give it all away. Chief of Staff Gabi Ashkenazi put his head down, clearly agreeing with the sentiment and abashed by the accusation. Tzipi Livni stirred uncomfortably. Prime Minister Ehud Olmert was caught off guard and stammered out a lame response. It made the front page of the newspapers the next day.

In relation to the prime minister's visit my commanders had given me a unique set of orders.

"You are to be part of a military entourage that will go with the Secret Service and ensure the safe exit of the prime minister and his helicopter."

"I'm not doing that," I replied defiantly. "There's a bus that arrives half an hour after his speech. He can take that."

My commander secretly agreed with my attitude, but he told me that I had to do it anyway. Half of my platoon was sent out in Hummers to an open area near the base. We dismounted the vehicles and spread out to ensure that no one would attack the prime minister during his exit. Just like a scene from Hollywood I watched his convoy of polished Lexus Land Cruisers roll up as two Black Hawk choppers descended from the sky. The prime minister boarded the chopper with his bodyguards, his expensive suit and tie flapping in the wind.

Back at the base we were all very upset by the prime minister's visit. It delayed lunch by three hours. In military culture this was clearly an unforgivable offense.

___

December 12th, 2008: Missile Ambushes

Previously I had been returning from a weekend leave and hopped on half a dozen different buses, making my way back to our base outside the Gaza Strip. I had been given a gift certificate to the local army surplus store and had no idea what to do with it. The certificate was about to expire. I perused the shelves but found nothing of interest or that I really needed.

Then I saw it. I didn't need it, and it had no real practical value. But I wanted it.

A machete`.

The gift certificate was just enough to purchase the blade. I picked it up and made my way back to the base outside of the Gaza Strip with machete` in hand.

Needless to say I received quite a few weird looks from people at the bus station in Beer Sheva. There I was, a combat Paratrooper, with an assault rifle in one hand and a machete` in the other. As I was about to board my bus, I saw a soldier in full uniform with another unusual object. It was a long stick with two weighted balls on each end.

"Okay, I have to ask," I inquired in Hebrew. "What is that thing?"

"It's a stick," he replied matter-of-factly.

"Well, that's obvious," I retorted. "What is it for?"

"I use it for juggling and other tricks."

"Um, okay," I replied with a raised eyebrow. "And what do you do in the IDF that requires you to carry a juggling stick around with you?"

"I'm an assistant to the colonel."

"Are you kidding me?" I asked, now switching to English. "You juggle for the colonel? Are you his personal court jester or something?"

He didn't really understand what I was saying but another Israeli couple did. They had to exit the line they were laughing so hard.

Axl had a genuine addiction to Coca-Cola. If I didn't know better I would have thought that he somehow managed to get a hold of the original recipe with cocaine in it. I also began drinking large amounts of the sugary beverage, but mainly because I needed the caffeine and Coca-Cola was usually easier to get than coffee.

It wasn't long before I figured out a way to rearrange my supplies in my combat vest to allow me to place a can of Coca-Cola in an ammunition pouch in my combat vest. This Coca-Cola came in handy on those long missions into the night and I needed a little bit of an extra kick.

One day my platoon was engaged in training in the *Achzeriot* (Armored Personnel Carriers). Bouncing along, a sharp metal corner apparently jabbed into my combat vest. Suddenly Axl noticed that he was becoming wet followed by a distinct hissing sound. Soon the commotion started after Axl realized that my coveted can of Coca-Cola in my combat vest had been punctured and was spewing sticky liquid all over the entire platoon.

"Get it out! Get it out!" They all yelled as I tore my equipment apart to open the ammunition pouch. With my left hand I lowered the top hatch and tossed the can out of the former-Russian tank with my right hand as if it had been a live hand grenade. Unfortunately, however, I had forgotten that this particular APC had been equipped with a glass bubble canopy on top. The can of Coca-Cola bounced off of the glass, dropped back down into the armored vehicle, and completely exploded, covering myself and my fellow sweating soldiers with the sticky, sugary liquid. Needless to say, I was very unpopular that day.

Immediately thereafter I realized that I needed to create some kind of "can protector." I soon found that cutting the cardboard tube of a potato chips can in half provided adequate protection.

Here in Paratroopers 890, *Mesayat*, we actually had quite a few Americans and other English-speaking immigrants. Two of my best friends were bald Americans, Chicken Fist and Cueball. One of these bald soldiers was coming into the unit and the other was leaving the same week. So there was only one obvious way to show my support and loyalty for both of them: shave my head completely bald.

We took "Before and After" videos and photos and then got a shot of the three bald Americans lined up. I also discovered that having no hair was actually much more comfortable with the helmet. It was a little bit cold, though. Also, to improve the deteriorating morale I went to drastic measures and gave my fellow soldiers a dry-erase marker and let them draw and write whatever they wanted on my head.

I was such a good friend.

Then with a variety of strange and profane words and drawings on my head I went to ask my commanders for spare gun oil, just to see their reaction. It was priceless. They had no idea what to do with me in the Israel Defense Force.

Lately we had been conducting SPIKE missile ambushes. I was usually part of a team that moved into secret positions just outside the fence and set up a missile launcher to take out select targets. I participated in five of these missile ambushes.

First Ambush: We moved into position perfectly. We were all set up and ready to go when I heard Sergeant Obama begin to curse. Apparently this wonderful sixty thousand dollar missile didn't work very well when he had forgotten the batteries to the viewing/targeting system.

We had to call the *Palchod* patrol to bring us the batteries. Not surprisingly, the *Palchod* weren't exactly discreet about it all and apparently our targets concluded that something was amiss and stayed in hiding.

Second Ambush: After arguing profusely to the officers about the wisdom of this ambush we were sent out anyway. The problem was that it was raining. There were several huge problems with doing any kind of ambush in the rain. This may be difficult to believe but Arabs had a unique cultural tendency that they only went to war when it was comfortable for them. This facet was especially true of untrained armies. This was a strange historical phenomenon common to all militant Moslem forces. The point was that if it was raining most terrorists would try to stay home even if they originally had plans to attack.

Also that same night the F-16's wouldn't go away, so our targets likewise stayed in hiding for that reason as well.

Third Ambush: After spending the entire night awake in the second ambush my commanders woke me up in the morning and I heard the alarms going off. Apparently a group of terrorists had opened fire on one of the *Palchod* patrols and *Palchod* had retaliated by opening the fence and going in after them. But it turned out to be a trap (big surprise) and the *Palchod* soldiers found themselves in a bit of a jam. They fought their way out of it but they scrambled multiple units in support. And we were sent out to set up a missile strike.

We flew on out to the fence in our Hummers and set up our position on a hill. Meanwhile, all hell had broken loose. Within *Mesayat* we had a sister platoon, Platoon Seven, that fired mortars from APC's.[1] The mortar crew received permission to fire and began to bombard targets in the Gaza Strip.

We lay on our hill watching the war. In front of us to the left we saw the mortars land, tanks moving in, and choppers flying. But then Sergeant Obama said to me, "Our orders are to take out targets… over there." He told me to find targets to the right of the landscape, where all was quiet and there was absolutely nothing happening.

Meanwhile, Axl was covering me and watching tanks move into the Gaza Strip with cannons booming. Then an Apache Gunship helicopter flew overhead and launched two hellfire missiles into a large building and blew it to pieces. All the while I was looking at a quiet part of the town for targets.

But then finally I found something. Two Hamas operatives were standing in a lookout point directing mortar fire. I locked on the missile and asked permission to fire.

Permission denied.

They themselves did not have weapons and were therefore not considered an official threat, even though they were directing the mortar fire. My response in English was a slightly more profane version of "You have got to be kidding me!"

After sitting on the hill for a while it became obvious that the Hamas operatives had seen us so we abandoned our ambush position. Ten minutes later after we had gone the terrorists commenced a heavy mortar bombardment of the hill.

When we got back to the base the colonel began yelling at me.

"Why didn't you kill them? They were directing the mortar fire!"

I just couldn't win in this army.

[1 This mortar system was called the *Keshet* (Rainbow/Arch) system and was a brand new development by the Israeli military. It was so new, in fact, that we were now beginning to sell prototypes to other militaries. It was my good friend and bald American, Chicken Fist (Z.H.), who entered history and was the first to fire this mortar system in a combat situation.]

Meanwhile, *Palchod* had been fighting off the terrorist ambush. Miraculously the *Palchod* patrol killed all four assaulting terrorists and sustained no casualties. However, the *Palchod* lieutenant in charge of the patrol, when all was said and done, accidentally blew off half of his hand by picking up one of the terrorists' loaded AK-47's by the barrel.

Likewise, the *Palchod* patrol used up all of their ammunition and grenades and was still sitting in the middle of the Gaza Strip. Upon their return the colonel chewed them out royally for not conserving their ammunition.

Fourth Ambush: As usual we made a proper entry and set up our position. This time we remembered the batteries but my commanders had failed to check to make sure that the power cord/adapter that connected the battery pack to the viewing/locking system actually worked. We had no choice but to use smaller batteries which were depleted sooner than we had been planning. It would be nice if my officers would make sure that all of the components of these sixty thousand dollar missiles actually worked ahead of time.

Fifth Ambush: We were in position, ready to go, with *working* missiles. And then we saw possible targets. In the thermal viewer we saw a group of people sitting in the area where Hamas usually placed their recon forces. Intel called it in to us and we confirmed seeing the same thing in our thermal vision. Likewise, we noticed a few other persons wandering in the same area. Now all we needed was for them to show themselves to be hostile in any way, or at least make it obvious they were Hamas operatives, and we could blow them halfway to the Suez Canal. Our two main targets were just sitting there. But then on a nearby road known for a high level of terrorist activity we saw a group of persons. They were quickly traveling down the road at a distance of about two kilometers away. They drew nearer and nearer to us. I prepared the missile and locked on, waiting for the order to shoot.

"Alright, Killswitch, be ready." Captain America whispered, showing excitement that we would finally have the opportunity to do what we came here for. "Stay locked on, be prepared to fire."

I watched the group come closer through the thermal vision.

"Um, Captain America," I began as I scrutinized the shapes on the thermal screen more closely. "It's a pack of stray dogs."

Disappointed, I returned to the original two targets, the sitting recon personnel. We discovered after a while that, although they were almost definitely human, they weren't moving... at all. And, over the course of the night, their body

189

temperature steadily dropped. It seemed apparent that they were already dead. Evidently we had just discovered two corpses half-frozen and rotting in the moonlight.

I didn't know who killed them, but it wasn't me. Had Hamas set them there in a morbid attempt to draw out our forces?

Then they sent us on a different type of ambush mission. It was not a missile ambush, but rather we set up a kill squad. This mission, however, was not a well thought-out plan. But then again, in my humble opinion most of our missions weren't well thought-out. The idea was that we were to actually cross the fence and enter the Gaza Strip. About four hundred meters from the Arab villages there was a wadi known for terrorist activity. They sent ten soldiers, with me in the front, to cut and cross the fence in the darkness, pass through an area known for mines and improvised explosive devices, sit on the edge of a wadi, and eliminate any and all terrorist threats that entered the wadi. But there were a few huge problems. First of all, it didn't take a genius to figure out that walking through an area replete with explosives wasn't the safest idea. But even more than that what was supposed to happen after we opened up fire to take out the terrorists? Due to the geography and large amounts of barb wire it took at least twenty minutes to get past the fence and back into friendly territory. I feared what would happen if we actually shot a terrorist in the Gaza Strip. I knew from personal experience we would suddenly realize that he had about a thousand friends that were eating, sleeping, or whatever else in their houses until they heard the gun shots. Then they would grab their AK-47's and try to hunt us down. And if it took us twenty minutes to evacuate the area then it was it was a recipe for disaster.

To make it worse, right before this mission I had just finished reading the book version of the movie, "Black Hawk Down."

The whole night before we conducted special training exercises in preparation for this mission. This also wasn't a smart idea, in my opinion, because we were exhausted by the time we went on the actual mission the following night.

Immediately before the mission we had a briefing with the major. The major, however, decided to ask us completely irrelevant questions. He called Axl up to the front of the room and said to him, "All of your commanders are dead. You need to call in a mortar strike on a specific target. How do you do it and describe in detail the weapons system that the mortar teams use, particularly the detonation mechanism on the shells."

We all held that priceless "Um... what?" expression on our faces. We were the Paratroopers, and we were the anti-tank and anti-personnel missile crew. We were also one of the main kill squads. How were we supposed to know off the top of our heads specific and technical details about the mortar equipment? To my surprise he actually knew most of it. But I never understood why exactly we needed to describe the intricate workings of the brand-new technologically advanced *Keshet* (Rainbow/Arch) system, especially for this mission?

Finally we went out. As usual I had myself painted up in a combination of army fatigues and Goth make-up, including the black nails. We jumped on the Hummers and started making our way to the fence.

"Killswitch," Axl called to me over the noise of the Hummer engine. "If I get killed and the last thing I see is your ugly Goth face I'm going to come back from the dead and take you out with me."

We were dropped off and quietly moved by foot about a kilometer (half mile) to the fence. We also crawled through about two hundred feet of large drainage pipe. Then we arrived at the fence, cut it quietly, and entered. About fifty meters (sixty yards) after the fence there was a large amount of barb wire. We had to walk for quite a while to get around it. Then we finally found the opening and crossed through, continuing our way closer to the Arab villages and the targeted wadi. On the way we passed through the improvised mine field. At one point I kicked something metal.

It could have been a remotely-detonated mine, it could have been an unexploded mortar shell, it could have been the shell of an exploded Kassam rocket, it could have been a harmless metal bucket. I never determined what it was exactly. But I wasn't about to go back to find out.

Now we were coming close to the wadi. Then a Hamas operative on a motorcycle rode down a winding path and by coincidence shined his headlight in our direction. I hissed to Captain America and we all dove to the ground. And we waited to find out if he had seen us. He didn't.

After a tense journey we arrived at the wadi and set up our position. We were positioned outside the wadi in a wide "V" pattern. The cross-fire was phenomenal, but we didn't have much cover except for the darkness.

It was extremely cold. And the fact that I had no hair didn't help.

We sat there all night in the cold, in the darkness, in the silence. It was quite bizarre being that close to the Arab villages. I heard babies crying, muffled arguments in Arabic, sporadic machine gun fire, and occasionally even a mortar bombardment. But for us all was quiet.

After an uneventful night we abandoned our ambush just before dawn. There was no grand finale. But that was life in the IDF.

Almost every day they bombed us. They usually launched mortars at us but every so often we saw the Kassam rockets fly overhead. In the day I could see the trail of smoke. At night they looked like slow shooting stars.

There was even a terrorist who would attack us almost every day at the same time. Every morning he would get out of bed, presumably eat breakfast, look at his watch, kiss his wife goodbye, and attack our patrol at seven forty-five. At a quarter to eight every day our alarm would go off, giving the signal of "Hot Hammer" to indicate that our troops were being shot at. This individual would blast a few rounds from his AK-47 at the patrol, being out of range to do much effective damage, and then flee back to his home. Likewise, our troops would scramble in response, but the terrorist would usually be too far gone at that point for a counter-attack to be realistic. This trend continued for weeks. We could have set our watches to it. Finally the Israel Defense Force grew weary of this game and positioned a tank in waiting ambush. At the appointed hour the terrorist once again began his unsuccessful attack. But this time the tank simply shelled him and that was the end of his morning routine.

Cueball, one of my fellow designated marksman in Platoon Five, recently counter-attacked three terrorists trying to plant a bomb.[1] Not long after they reciprocated by mortaring a kibbutz and military base not far from mine. I tried calling my friends to find out what happened but everyone had their cell phones shut off. They were probably on response somewhere near the fence. I heard eight soldiers were wounded, some of them having had various appendages blown off.

Rumor had it, however, that these wounded soldiers were the excuse that the government had been waiting for, and that the cease-fire was finally over. We would see if there really was a war this time...

[1 The final report indicated that the terrorists were not killed. Accordingly, the platoon-commanding lieutenant was reprimanded for ordering Cueball and his partner to take the shot at too far of a range.]

December 28th, 2008: Tell Me That You Miss Me

It was early December, 2008. I hadn't gone home for a few weeks and I was scheduled for my normal weekend leave. My officers told me I could go home. I gave them an answer they never expected to hear.

"No."

They were in shock. In the history of the Israel Defense Force I doubted anyone had ever actually refused to go home.

"Um... Okay, Killswitch. Why exactly don't you want to go home?"

"I have no money and therefore I can't buy enough alcohol to keep myself drunk the entire weekend."

"Are you serious?" My officers asked incredulously.

"Yes, I am."

"But... Killswitch, you *have* to go home."

"I refuse. You can punish me by taking away my weekend leave and making me stay on base."

In the Israel Defense Force the basic form of punishment for direct disobedience to an officer was taking away his weekend leave. So what could they do when the offense was refusing to go home?

They gave up.

There was more to my refusal than a lack of alcohol, however. For one thing I knew that the cease-fire was about to end. It was scheduled to end mid-December. And if all hell broke loose I wanted to be on the line with my friends, not sitting around at home... sober. I also knew that if I did go home and the Gaza Strip went out of control they would just ruin my weekend leave and call me right back. And, according to army rules, if I was home for even two hours then that would be considered my weekend leave and they could legally lock me down on base for another month. I was trying to make a deal with them to allow me to take my weekend leave a week later after the situation with the cease-fire quieted down.

It was a little strange to admit but at this point I had become genuinely institutionalized. I didn't know how to survive without the military. I didn't feel normal or comfortable in society. I didn't want to see my friends. Even more so I was honestly embarrassed. I had been under orders essentially to allow terrorists to shoot RPG's and mortars at me for half a year. The morale of the entire battalion was crushed. I honestly was ashamed to get on a bus wearing the Israeli uniform. I couldn't describe how horrible I felt to put on the Paratrooper dress uniform and go home in a bus that passed through Ashkelon, watching the pillars of smoke rise into the sky from the falling rockets I was supposed to be stopping. And I wasn't allowed to do a thing about it.

Finally, however, towards the evening I decided I might as well go home. I hadn't been home in almost a month and I had a lot of things to do. And my laundry wouldn't wash itself.

I went home depressed more than ever. I knew that this was it. Golani (another combat unit, basically the "Northern Rangers") was already arriving on our base to replace us. We were on our way to the Golan Heights to conduct winter war exercises. I would participate in the war training for a few months, be on the front line on the Lebanese border, and then maybe be stationed near Ramallah in the West Bank for another couple of months. And that would be the end of my military service in the IDF. And what did I feel that I had accomplished? Nothing.

I arrived home late and went straight to bed. I got up the next morning and did my normal routine of trying to get stuff done. I was very happy, however, to discover my secret alcohol stash.[1] I visited the dormitory of a group of my female friends participating in a religious study program on my kibbutz. I was particularly interested in a certain girl named Cocoa Puff. She was a gorgeous Costa Rican girl and the chemistry had already begun to build. We spent a lot of time together. Later that night I visited her and her friends at the dormitory. I was also highly intoxicated.

Then Axl called me.

" 'ello?" I slurred.

"Hey, buddy. Are you drunk?" My good friend asked, knowing the obvious

[1] I had discovered that if I hid alcohol for myself when I was drunk I didn't remember where it was and stumbled upon it only in a time of severe sobriety and therefore emergency.]

answer.

"Of course," I replied matter-of-factly.

"I thought you were out of alcohol."

"So did I, but I foun' some."

"Have you heard about what's happening?" He changed the topic.

"No."

"The whole Gaza Strip has gone to hell."

I started laughing hysterically. The Israeli government in its infinite wisdom never thought that when the "cease-fire" ended Hamas might actually think that the "cease-fire" was over.

Why didn't anybody ever listen to me?

Then my lieutenant, Captain America, called me.

"Captain America!" I yelled into the phone much louder than necessary. "The cease-fire is over."

"Yes, I know," he responded.

"Are you callin' me to come back to base?"

"Yes."

"I knew it!" I laughed. "I told you so! Was I right or was I right?"

"Killswitch, are you drunk?" Captain America also asked the obvious question.

"Yes, I am!" I declared proudly.

"I thought you were out of alcohol."

"So did I, but then I foun' some. Nevermind. I'm tired of tellin' that story. Anyway, Captain America, I will come back to base but only *after* you tell me that *you miss me!*"

"Um, Killswitch," Captain America hesitated. "I'm not going to tell you that. I am going to say that you are my best soldier, you are my lead designated marksman, and I need you."

"No! That's not good enough! Tell me that you *miss* me!" I demanded.

"Killswitch," I heard a heavy sigh on the other end of the line. "Okay, fine. I miss you. Come back to base."

"Aw, how sweet! Do you *really* miss me?"

"Killswitch, you're really starting to push it," my officer warned.

"Okay, okay. I'll come back to base on the first bus in the morning."

Apparently I also called Sergeant Obama in the middle of the night, but I had no recollection of that.

First thing in the morning I returned to my base outside of the Gaza Strip.

And... Nothing was happening. Or, rather, we were still under orders not to respond to any kind of attack. The entire Gaza Strip was engulfed in violence. We were being bombed, as usual. And I had been ordered to end my blissful insobriety for no apparent reason.

Not long after we were given a mission. Intel had picked up that Hamas was planning some kind of large attack at a certain point near a large trash dump. I went out there with Sergeant Obama and we set up our SPIKE missiles and waited. There were several other groups of soldiers as well, including snipers and a handful of tanks.

Then, at the appropriate time, a set of large trucks made their way toward us. I readied the missile and locked on. In the end, however, they turned out to be just a trash crew dumping waste at the dump. I could only imagine what they thought when they arrived at the dump and noticed several tank cannons pointed at them.

In a moment of frustration I thought about how much fun it would be to "accidentally" launch a missile into the huge mountain of trash that composed their "dump." To have seen the explosion and massive quantities of airborne waste floating across the Gaza Strip would have been priceless. But I restrained myself. Besides, knowing the level of criticism that the IDF faced it would have probably been some kind of "war crime." I was sure that some anti-Semitic lawyer somewhere in the world would have found some vague clause in the Fourth Geneva Convention that such an action would have violated.

A few days later we were given another mission. We were having problems with a Palestinian sniper. A terrorist had gotten a hold of a legendary Dragonuv 7.62mm sniper rifle. From a range of over a kilometer (half a mile) he had hit the driver's side door of one of our patrols, barely missing the driver himself.

We were determined to take him out. The problem was that we didn't know exactly who he was or where he was. And we were still not permitted to enter the Gaza Strip itself. It became a game of cat-and-mouse with a kilometer (half a mile) of No Man's Land separating us.

We had devised a sophisticated plan to eliminate this sniper, but for security reasons I couldn't disclose it. But at the last minute they canceled our mission. To make it worse even with all of the Gaza Strip degenerating into chaos the Israeli government declared a forty-eight hour period of absolutely no aggression against anything or anyone in the Gaza Strip. They could shoot at us all day long and even walk up to the fence holding an RPG and wait for our patrol and we weren't allowed to do *anything*.

We were all *really* upset. I'll never forget the look on Captain Crunch's face when he gave us the briefing. He hung his head with extreme embarrassment and humiliation.

It was a Friday night, December 26th, the day before my Gregorian birthday. I was angry and depressed. I resigned myself to the unfortunate truth that my military career would end in six months and I would have done nothing significant at all.

The next day it was about eleven thirty in the morning. It was December 27th and my birthday. It was *Shabbat* morning and I was talking with Cueball and my other new American friend, Rambo, after praying in the synagogue.

The entire base shook from a series of enormous explosions. I had never seen or felt anything like it. The whole base degenerated into chaos. There had been no "Purple Rain" incoming bombardment alarm so no one had any idea what was going on. My friends and I ran full-speed back to our rooms and suited up with our body army, helmets, and combat vests as quickly as possible. To my surprise some of the soldiers in my platoon were still sleeping.

"What is wrong with you?!" I yelled at the slumbering soldiers. "Wake up! We're getting bombed like never before!"

It didn't take long for them to hear the deafening rumbling and feel the ground shake.

But there was still no alarm.

I ran fully-equipped to the nearby "shelter." Once again the *jobnik* girls were sitting there and crying. For a brief moment I thought about telling them to "man up." But then I realized that they were just eighteen year-old little girls working administrative jobs on the base and to have said such a thing would have been incredibly insensitive, even for me. I softened my criticism and ignored them.

We started up the Hummers and prepared the response teams. Somehow in my Hummer there wasn't enough room for me.

"Killswitch," Sergeant Obama called to me. "There's not enough room. You need to stay here."

"Over my dead body!"

I wasn't really sure what was going on, but I would sooner shoot myself than sit in a shelter with crying teenage girls. Then Captain Crunch told me there was room in one of the Hummers of Platoon Five.

"I'll take it!" I agreed.

"Killswitch!" Sergeant Obama called to me as I climbed into other Humvee. "What is that strapped to your back?"

"My machete`," I replied simply.

"You are not normal..." Sergeant Obama muttered but his voice was soon drowned out by the roar of the Hummer engines.

I snatched a seat on the Hummer next to my South African friend, Weeman. I popped open a can of Coca-Cola and rode out to the fence.

We arrived near the fence and waited for orders. It was then that our officers informed us of what was going on. Our own government had lied to us (not that this should have been that big of a surprise). The Israeli government had issued a two-day cease-fire to give Hamas "one final chance" to renew the peace. Hamas was told, as usual, that if they violated the cease-fire we would retaliate.

As usual Hamas ignored our warnings. And for the first time in a very long time we actually did something about it. The moment they started firing missiles into Israel our air force commenced heavy bombardment of select targets. But nobody told us that. The bombing was so intense that we thought the Palestinian Arabs were bombing our base again. In reality it was our air force bombing them.[1]

Not long after we heard the command given over the radio. We had received the green light for what would soon be dubbed "Operation: Cast Lead." Soon we would be going into the Gaza Strip.

It was *Shabbat*. Normally on *Shabbat* I didn't use my phone. But this was a special occasion. It was the beginning of a war and we were in the military. I called Axl to let him know that he needed to come back to base. We were so happy! Finally we had a war! We had been sitting around and getting bombed for half a year, not to mention the eight years of continual rocket and missile attacks on the southern portions of Israel. Almost eight thousand rockets, missiles, and mortars had already landed on Israeli targets, the vast majority of them being civilian. It should also be noted that the areas under attack were not "disputed territories." Even according to the 1948 UN Partition and the 1993 Oslo Accords the areas suffering from mortar, rocket, and missile assaults were one hundred percent Jewish land. And as soldiers we were simply tired of not being allowed to retaliate. Now, finally, we could do something about it.

Even my friend Cocoa Puff called me. She also didn't normally use the phone on *Shabbat*. She was staying on our kibbutz for the weekend. But it wasn't long before she heard the alarms and distant booming. Likewise, several of the kibbutz residents themselves threw on uniforms and jumped in cars, returning to the army during their weekend leave or having been called up in the reserves. She knew something big was happening.

But at the moment we were just waiting. We didn't respond immediately. By now it was evening. We were monitoring Hamas movements when one of our tanks rolled by on a patrol. Apparently Hamas tried to mortar the tank, but the

[1] This series of airstrikes on Saturday, December 27th, 2008, would later be dubbed by Palestinian Arabs as "Black Saturday." Over one hundred targets were initially hit simultaneously in the space of less than four minutes. The Israel Air Force boasted over ninety-five percent accuracy. Half an hour later an additional sixty aircraft conducted a second sweep. It was allegedly the deadliest attack against Palestinian Arab militants during over sixty years of the Israeli-Palestinian conflict.]

shell landed a lot closer to us, about forty meters (one hundred and fifty feet) away.

That was what I hated most about mortars. I didn't know when they were coming or where they were coming from and therefore I couldn't shoot back. Just as we were trying to determine where the next mortar would land I saw a huge blast, almost like a mushroom cloud, in the distance. And just like delayed thunder the sound of the impact followed ten seconds later. Our air force had hit them again.

Not long after I saw the eerie glow of a Kassam flying out of the Gaza Strip. The entire region echoed with the alarms. The warning system consisted of a cold, feminine voice calmly declaring *"Tzeva Adom* (Color Red)." Here all the alarms of various kibbutzim and Jewish population centers sounded simultaneously. The civilian residents had five to seven seconds to find shelter. Sure enough, a blinding flash of light, as if from a giant camera, came after the missile had been launched, indicating its impact on an Israeli civilian target. And then the boom followed, also delayed like distant thunder.

We returned to the base and started pulling out all of our war equipment. Additionally, Captain America chose me to assist him as part of a three-man response team to various threats on the border. At all hours of the night we would hop out to selected spots on the fence to take out suspected threats.

It was about eight in the morning. We had responded to a threat consisting of at least one terrorist in a group of bushes between his car and a small house.

I arrived at our pillbox just outside the fence bordering Israel and the Gaza Strip. Captain American and I climbed up to the top floor and set up the launcher on the roof as quickly as possible, trying to keep our heads down from snipers. After the launcher was in place I climbed onto the small roof of the pillbox and began operating the system. Then an argument began. The colonel of Paratroopers 890 as well as the Southern-Command general wanted us to shoot the missile.

Supposedly there was a terrorist in a fifty meter (about one hundred and eighty feet) patch of thick shrubbery. These bushes were situated between a building and a small, white car. They told me to fire a missile into the bushes, hopefully in the general area of the terrorist.

"You've got to be kidding me!" I muttered under my breath. This sixty thousand dollar missile was a precise weapon and not designed for such an attack. If they wanted to destroy the entire patch of shrubbery and anything and everything in it they needed to call in an air strike or a mortar strike.

Captain American likewise complained, stressing that we did not have a clear target.

They told us to fire anyway. I entered into the launching system and prepared to fire. About that time the Arab terrorists figured out we were on top of the pillbox and began to mortar us. A large boom from a distance of a mere thirty meters (one hundred feet) distracted me.

"Killswitch! Stay focused!" Captain America admonished.

"Yeah, easy for you to say," I scowled. I then asked, "Do I have permission to fire?"

"Permission *Granted.*"

I fired the missile. The missile landed in the patch of bushes with a large explosion.

"Wow..." I exclaimed. "That was actually really cool."

"Killswitch! Fire another one!" My lieutenant ordered.

"You got it!" I replied excitedly.

I launched another missile into the bushes, now more certain of where the target was supposed to be. But this time the guiding system malfunctioned and it didn't land exactly in the patch of bushes where I had wanted it. Later I wished I had aimed at the car so that, when the guiding system failed, I would have "accidentally" sent their little white Renault halfway back to France.

Apparently we didn't hit the terrorists, but this action was the first offensive action taken by ground troops of Operation: Cast Lead. Therefore according to official record I fired the first shots of ground troops of the conflict and commenced the ground aspects of the operation.

We returned to the base after our response. Before I even got there everyone already knew what had happened and made sure to ridicule me about it as much as possible. Everywhere I went in the IDF after that incident somebody would come up to me and ask, "Hey, aren't you that American guy that wasted over one hundred thousand dollars blowing up some bushes?"

We packed up our war equipment as quickly as possible and proceeded to a staging point near Beer Sheva in the south. While there I received a phone call from an old friend of mine that I knew back in Arizona. He was also here in Israel. He was hired by Chabad, an international Chassidic Jewish religious organization, to write blogs and journal entries for their website. They asked him if he knew any soldiers that would be interested in keeping a short blog on their website. So he called me. I agreed.

I began writing the blog for Chabad. At first I used my cell phone to send text/sms messages as well as to access the internet and sent my entries to my Chabad contact via Facebook. Later, however, this method proved to be inadequate. And in the initial assault itself they locked away our cell phones.

After my friend called me about writing the blog several officers I didn't recognize came up to me.

"Are you Sergeant Killswitch?" They inquired in a business-like manner.

"Yeah," I affirmed. "Who wants to know and why?"

"Is it true that you wasted over one hundred thousand dollars of missiles today blowing up bushes?"

These officers had come specifically to investigate me and my expensive landscaping techniques. And they were not happy. In the end nothing happened to me. I had been ordered by a general and a colonel to fire them. But this was the military, and it was easier to cause problems for the little guy, i.e., me. And this was the Jewish Army after all. Such a waste of resources would not go unnoticed.

PART VIII: OPERATION: CAST LEAD

December 29th, 2008: Why I Was Fighting

Today we received our orders. That was about all I could say. Initially there was a wave of excitement but then it became a sobering time. I couldn't describe what it was like to look at the faces of my closest friends and wonder which of them would die. I was twenty-four, but most of them were only nineteen or twenty. They were just kids. Many of them looked to me for support, being older and more experienced with death. But there wasn't a lot I could say. My usual response was to laugh it off with a dark, twisted joke and show no fear myself. Honestly, I wasn't that scared. I was too stupid to be scared.

I lived on a religious kibbutz in the south. For the first time Grad missiles issued by the Soviet military were landing a few kilometers (miles) away from my home. One of my closest friends, Cocoa Puff, called me from a bomb shelter. She was shaking. When I made Aliyah I was fighting for a Jewish ideal. When I joined the Paratroopers I was fighting for the State of Israel. But now... I was fighting for my home, for my friends, for myself.

December 30th, 2008: Surprise Visitors

Last night was the eighth and final night of Chanukah. I had been sent to a nearby base for preparation. While organizing and checking equipment I looked up to the sound of music. I laughed with surprise as the world-famous Chabad Chanukah mobile arrived, complete with a giant, glowing *Chanukiah* (menorah for Chanukah). There, amidst incoming bombs and alarms, with soldiers scurrying to and fro with machine guns and missile launchers, the *Chabadnikim* (Chassidic Jews) started passing out *Tehillim* (Psalms), *siddurim* (prayer books), and Chanukah goodies. And after days of eating tuna and Loof the value of Chanukah doughnuts and chocolate *gelt* skyrocketed.

Then the soldiers started dancing with more energy than I had ever seen at any wedding or *Bar Mitzvah*. Maybe it was because we knew that for some of us it would be our last dance.

I looked on the whole scene and smiled. It was nice to know we were not alone. In that place I realized more than ever before what a unique place Israel was, and that the Jewish people working together was an amazing thing.

I felt myself qualified to say on behalf of Paratroopers 890 a very special thank you to Chabad. They definitely made our night.

December 31st, 2008: A Friendly Brawl

Tonight was New Year's Eve, or so they told me. It was also my Hebrew birthday. It was nine in the evening and I was exhausted from a full day of touch-up training. The Heavy Weapons & Recon Company of Paratroopers 890 was legendary for being slightly rogue. And tonight the officers made the mistake of placing well over a hundred Paratroopers, all from rival companies, together in the same small hangar. First it started with a singing match, each company trying to shout their respective songs louder than the other. But after a while it went a little too far. Suddenly fruit, vegetables, and toilet paper started to fly across the hangar. I put my earphones in and pulled my sleeping bag over my head. At twenty-four I considered myself "too old" for the antics of nineteen year-old kids. Besides, I never really understood the rivalry.

For my Non-Jewish New Year and my Hebrew birthday there was no kosher steak, no kosher beer, and no beautiful kosher women. There was simply an oxymoronic "friendly brawl" in a hangar.

January 1st, 2009: Soldiers Running

While organizing our equipment (again!) I was startled by an outbreak of shouting and a large pack of soldiers running in a single direction.

"What happened?" I yelled over the confusion. "Incoming missiles? Emergency alert?"

No... Donations!

The moment I heard that I also joined the stampede of soldiers to be the first in line to get free stuff.

Friends of the IDF had arrived with an impressive entourage of donors. The donors were mostly American, particularly the Jewish president of a large chain of domestic and home accessory stores. These individuals had left their busy and successful lives in the United States simply to personally express their gratitude to us even before we embarked on our military operation. And, of course, they brought with them a much appreciated collection of donated goods ranging from winter clothing to delicious edibles. They pulled me and a few other American *chayalim bodedim* (lone soldiers) aside.

"My mom just loves your towels," my friend addressed the commercial president.

I rolled my eyes and shook my head.

"Smooth, dude. Really smooth," I thought to myself. But evidently my friend meant it as a joke and the CEO laughed.

I also met a rabbi from my home town who was a regional vice president for Friends of the IDF. With us Jews it was always a small world. He was very warm and friendly. I could see in his eyes that his concern for us was very genuine, not just a gimmick for the sake of appearances.

I couldn't emphasize enough how much we appreciated the support, especially when the entire world was criticizing us. And we hadn't even done anything yet! It amazed me the amount of anti-Semitism and condemnation already hurled at the State of Israel and we hadn't even started the attack beyond air strikes.

January 3rd, 2009: There Was No "Tomorrow"

Apparently this was it. Since last *Shabbat* we had been on maximum alert and waiting for the order to initialize the ground assault. And every day for the past week they had been telling us, "Tomorrow! For sure tomorrow!"

So every day our nerves had been on edge. But now there was no "tomorrow."

The state that the Gaza Strip had reached was unbelievable. At this point the number of mines, tunnels, and booby traps there was astounding. And according to the press Hamas had legalized crucifixion and they were setting up crosses in Gaza.[1] There was so much death in the Gaza Strip that hundreds of vultures circled overhead incessantly.

I realized that there was a strong possibility, even an unfortunate likelihood, that this would have been the end of my writings.

I thought about the twenty-four years of my life. My life had been far from perfect but I had no regrets. I had lived life to the fullest, to a fault even.

With me there were no frantic pleas to G-d for forgiveness, nor was there a desperate begging for survival. Rather, it was more of a calm acceptance of fate.

About the time of my *Bar Mitzvah* I had made a pledge to do whatever I could to defend the Jewish people and, if possible, to do so with the IDF Paratroopers. Eleven years later here I was.

We all have dreams. Only a small few of us are privileged enough to realize them.

So if I survived this I would have lived my dream. If I didn't, then I would die next to my best friends doing what I had always wanted to do. I felt that I was privileged to take part in a legacy that began with Avraham rescuing his nephew, Lot, and Simeon and Levi retrieving their sister, Dinah. And that legacy

[1] I found this rumor difficult to believe initially. I later did check into it and verified that it was true. Just a few days after Christmas, 2008, Hamas passed the *Shari'a* criminal code. Among other things this Code did legalize the nailing of "enemies of Islam" to crosses for the purposes of a crucifixion. How nice it was to see Hamas get into the holiday spirit!]

was taking great risks to defend the Jewish people.

For me there were no more politics. I was not a hero. I was a twenty-four year-old Jewish pharmacy technician, banker, and aspiring writer that disliked missiles falling on his apartment and his friends sitting in bomb shelters.

I had only one prayer. That, live or die, I would not fail the Jewish people. And even more importantly, that I would not fail my friends.

Today the whole world would be watching me. One hundred years from now people would talk of this day and write about it. And on this day I was happy.

We were going into the Gaza Strip. Paratroopers 890 went in first. And I, with the Heavy Weapons & Recon Company, had already started the show and would continue to do so.

And so it began...

Day 1. January 3rd, 2009: Entering the Gaza Strip

It was four-thirty in the afternoon. The sun was beginning the first stage of setting. The whole battalion sat in an auditorium listening attentively to the final speech delivered by the colonel. Suddenly his speech was interrupted. The entire building rocked and the windows shook violently from a massive explosion. There was a moment of silence but the colonel merely smiled and looked at his watch.

"That's our air force," he explained. "And they are starting exactly on time, just as they promised."

The tension broke. That was when I realized more than ever that the war was real. The war was here.

After the briefing we made a final check on our equipment and painted our faces with camouflage paint. I then placed a purple bandana on my head pirate-style. This bandana was a source of teasing for the entire war. The bandana was a gift from one my good friends who was a married religious woman. I had been hanging out with her, Cocoa Puff, and the rest of their woman's religious study group. We drank a few *L'Chaims* (toasts) and for some unknown reason I really wanted the bandana. It seemed like a good idea at the time. She happily gave it to me, and my female friends all wrote nice messages on it. I soon discovered, however, that the bandana itself was extremely comfortable underneath my helmet. It provided warmth in cold weather and absorbed sweat in hot weather. And, of course, I didn't settle for merely camouflage face paint. I once again used my Goth corpse paint complete with lip liner, eye liner, black fingernail polish, etc. With my face painted and a purple bandana on my head I proceeded to put on my helmet, body armor, combat vest, and a backpack designed to carry two SPIKE missiles. I later weighed the missile pack and found that it came in at over forty-five kilograms (one hundred pounds).

I was in Platoon Six. Our task was to enter the Gaza Strip from the very north relatively close to the beach. We were to proceed three kilometers by foot to a hill on the outskirts of Elei Sinai. Elei Sinai was a dismantled Jewish village similar to Gush Katif[i] that once existed in the Gaza Strip. Now it was reduced to chunks of concrete and abandoned roads.

We left the base. Ironically as we left we had to wait in line and sign-in.

"Hey, Axl," I called to my best friend. "Are we going to a war or a wedding?"

[¹ Gush Katif was a controversial village in the Gaza Strip. It was originally built in 1930 on land bought from the Arabs in an area called Kfar Drom. Later it was evacuated in 1948 when the Egyptians took over the Gaza Strip. In 1967 Egypt lost control of the Strip and in 1968 the Jews began to return. The Palestinian Arabs, however, were very upset about this and demanded their expulsion, even though the Jewish return was in complete accordance with the Fourth Geneva Convention. Later in 1993 in the Oslo Accords even Yasir Arafat agreed that the area was indeed Jewish land, especially since the Jews living there still held the title deeds. The Oslo Accords allowed the Jews to remain in their homes. However, in August of 2005 then Prime Minister Ariel Sharon and the Israeli government complied with international pressure, forcing eight thousand Jews out of their homes. Some of the Jews refused to comply with the orders, and the military was sent in to forcibly evacuate them. It became a near civil war because a significant portion of the Israel Defense Force also refused to comply. (If I had been there, I wouldn't have done it either). Eventually the Jews were driven out and the towns destroyed. Gush Katif was worth over twenty-three billion dollars in combined assets. When the area was given away to the Palestinian Arabs what little was left they further destroyed. And Hamas turned the residential areas into a terrorist training camp. The Israeli economy and political mindset suffered indefinitely from the Gush Katif expulsion. All throughout his term President Barack Obama and the international community wanted us to do the same thing in the West Bank. In Gush Katif there were eight thousand Jews. In the West Bank there were over three hundred thousand Jews. The idea of removing all Jews from the West Bank was simply a highly unrealistic solution. It would start a civil war and utterly destroy the economy of both the State of Israel as well as the "disputed territory" of the West Bank. It was important to realize that over sixty percent of the Palestinian Arab economy was directly tied to the Israeli economy and the "troublesome settlements." Therefore even the notion of boycotting Israeli goods in an attempt to support Palestinian Arabs was highly counterproductive, probably hurting the Palestinian Arabs more than the Israeli Jews. Additionally, the so-called "settlements" were usually fully developed cities and suburbs and the land was both traditionally Jewish land as well as usually purchased long before 1948. Hebron, for example, was the site of the grave of our patriarch Avraham, and was even the capital of the Kingdom of Israel for a brief period of time. There never had been a country or kingdom called "Palestine," and no other people could make such a claim. Hebron, however, was a hotly disputed area and it was the firm opinion of the United Nations and President Barack Obama that all Jews should be forcibly expelled.]

Finally we started moving. And then the bombardment began with Platoon Seven specializing as a state-of-the-art *Keshet* mortar crew. I had seen bombardment before, but nothing like this. This time they brought out the big guns. The mortars themselves made huge mushrooms of fire and the following boom resonated throughout the entire landscape.

The moment the bombardment began all nervousness vanished. I no longer felt alone, like a measly infantry soldier in the Paratroopers weighed down by missiles. We were a team. We were an army. We were friends. And we were going to take down Hamas.

The air force also accompanied us. At almost all times there were Apache gunship choppers flying overhead as well as drone aircraft hovering in support. Likewise, the landscape was occasionally illuminated by an enormous explosion in the distance. It was only then that I would hear the sonic roar of the F-15 Eagles flying low overhead afterwards followed by the impact of the detonation.

We pressed on. What they didn't tell us, however, was that the entire distance consisted of sand dunes. Walking three kilometers (two miles) in sand dunes with two missiles, body armor, a twenty-four hour supply of food and water, two hundred bullets, and more, was not the most fun thing in the world.

It was *so* cold. Anyone who thought that Israel was consistently warm and pleasant was in serious error. The climate was very similar to southern California. In the summer it was warm, even hot, especially in the deserts. But in the winter it became cold, mainly because of the proximity to the sea. And tonight apparently was not an exception.

Finally we reached our destination and prepared to set up shop with Platoon Five, the Recon Platoon, on a ridge in Elei Sinai. This ridge overlooked the first towns of the Gaza Strip from where most of the Kassam rockets had been launched at Israeli civilians. When we arrived, however, the colonel reassessed the situation and realized that the vast majority of the targets that we were supposed to destroy with our SPIKE missiles had fled from the air force and mortars. So there was no real reason for us to stay there with the Recon Platoon as originally planned. Therefore we were ordered to continue south and join Platoon Eight as a light infantry force spearheading the operation. The only problem was that we still had the missiles and other equipment on our backs, and we had just been ordered to walk another seven kilometers (four miles). Needless to say it was a nightmare. That was the longest seven kilometers (four miles) I had ever walked in my life, and I strongly suspected that it was significantly longer than that.

We continued marching... and marching... and marching. All the while the mortars and air force proceeded to blow up almost everything in front of us. Apparently the idea of the bombing was not just to clear our path but also to make sure that no civilians remained in the area. The explosions were so enormous that even from a distance of a kilometer (half a mile) I could feel a solid rush of air against my face and my ears popped from the sudden change of pressure. Now imagine that a person was sitting in their house, stubbornly refusing to evacuate, and then mortars started landing fifty meters from their backyard. The idea was that anyone willing to stay in the area after that kind of bombardment was either a terrorist ready for a fight and/or suicidal. The technique worked quite well, and most of the urban areas we entered were almost completely void of civilian life. This fact was completely contrary, of course, to what the media would have the world believe.

At about five in the morning we arrived at our new destination. It was an abandoned orchard just outside the first city. We quickly dug in and waited for the sun to rise and the rest of the Israeli armed forces to catch up. It was so cold I couldn't feel my feet and I was actually worried that I had a serious problem. Likewise, I think most of us had mild hypothermia because some of us, including myself, started passing out while standing up. Later I heard that at least six soldiers from a sister battalion had to be evacuated from severe hypothermia.

I also heard that the Golani battalion had walked into a booby trap. Golani had entered the assault more from a southern and diagonal angle, if one was to consult a map. Golani, however, was known for entering combat quickly and sometimes even recklessly. In some situations this feature served to be an advantage. In the Gaza Strip, however, it proved to be detrimental. The Paratroopers had proceeded slightly slower, with our mortars (hopefully) detonating any mines, explosives, or other booby traps along the way. Apparently Golani moved in too fast, or their mortars had missed something. They stepped on a very large mine. Two of their soldiers died and twenty of them were wounded.

Day 2. January 4th, 2009: Snipers, Mortars, and Missiles

The sun rose, for which I was quite thankful. In my mind sunlight logically equaled warmth, which was a very welcome idea at the moment. I then began to survey my surroundings in the daylight. To the east and south were the beginnings of a town. I was surprised, however, to see sparkling blue Mediterranean water to the west. I knew we were close to the beach, but I didn't realize how close.

We remained in our foxholes waiting for the rest of the IDF to catch up. Late that morning I heard a distant cracking noise followed by low, dull buzzing noises similar to angry hornets flying around our heads.

It was sniper fire.

I dove back into my foxhole and cautiously peered over the edge with my M4 assault rifle and Trijicon scope, trying to determine where the bullets were coming from. A nearby tank, however, identified the source of enemy fire before I did. A few well-placed tank shells in his building ended his relatively short-lived career as a Hamas sniper. He wasn't the only one, however, and we continued this pattern for most of the day.

Somewhere about lunchtime I actually began paying attention to the orchard itself. The trees themselves were fruitless, but they were surrounded by greenery that I originally thought were merely weeds. In reality they were peas; nice, fresh peas in a pod. They were abandoned, forlorn, lonely... and delicious. So Axl and I spent the whole day sitting in a foxhole, taking fire from an occasional sniper, and eating peas. The thought did occur to me that it seemed a tad bit inconsistent that the Gazan Arabs complained of a lack of food and I had just found an abandoned orchard full of produce.

Then nightfall came. As soon as the sun set we made our way to a nearby make-shift logistics center to resupply. While refilling our water and food as well as *finally* getting rid of the missiles we heard a burst of nearby gunfire. The shots were followed by a commander from a sister platoon screaming and collapsing to the ground. I readied my rifle and scanned through my night vision scope for the threat. But it wasn't enemy fire. It was a freak accident. Somehow the 7.62mm MAG machine gun mounted on an *Achzerit* armored personnel carrier went off and hit the commander in the chest three times at point blank range. To my shock he survived. Miraculously his ceramic body armor stopped all three bullets. I was quite surprised because the body armor was not supposed to be strong enough to stop 7.62mm rounds at that close of range. He suffered a few

217

cracked ribs and a punctured lung. But he survived and he would eventually have a full recovery.

Now we assaulted the town itself. Once again the bombardment began. Either it was heavier than before or, more likely, we were simply a much closer to the falling shells and rockets. I particularly marveled at the ATG (air-to-ground) rockets fired from the choppers. They made a strange, almost science-fiction noise as they descended from the sky. And there was nothing, and I mean *nothing*, like an incoming Hellfire missile.

It was definitely a show. No amount of television or video games could prepare me for it. It was simply an overload of all my senses. I felt the rumbling in my body. My ears popped from the pressure. I smelled the sulfur and burnt flesh. In one house in particular several Hamas operatives tried to make a stand. One incendiary missile ended that endeavor. I remained crouched behind a half-destroyed building watching the flames lick the night sky and hearing the terrorists scream. The explosion itself hadn't killed at least one of the Hamas men. He was now half-crushed and burning alive with no hope of survival.

We pressed forward. We ourselves, the Paratroopers, encountered little resistance. Hamas was unable to stand against the mortars and air force. We continued moving and ultimately took over a small neighborhood known for Hamas activity. We entered the first house. Normally I was partnered with the platoon-commanding lieutenant, Captain America, and kicked the door in and went in first. The platoon was divided into two squads: the lead squad and the missile squad. For this operation, however, Sergeant Obama requested to change the order a little bit and made me the lead missile specialist as well as the lead designated marksman of the second squad. It had its advantages and disadvantages. It was definitely more my style to kick all the doors in, but in the second squad I was partnered with my best friend Axl as well as the head sergeant.

Once again we had worked all night and now it was near daybreak, so we fortified ourselves in one of the Hamas leader's houses. Again we waited for dawn and the rest of the army to catch up. It was then that I discovered that now the plumbing in the house no longer worked. And when there were over thirty soldiers from two platoons stationed in one house for a long period of time with no working toilets... it was a bad scene.

Day 3. January 5th, 2009: Booby Traps and Tuna Soufflé

We continued conquering building after building. In the afternoon we moved out after tossing a few smoke grenades to cover our advance. Resistance was still minimal. But now we ran into a different problem: booby traps.

We had taken control of a small apartment building. While I continued with Sergeant Obama and Axl to clear out each floor Captain America advanced with his squad to clear out a neighboring building. Intel had told us that there was a very large mine buried in the road. Captain America placed about a kilogram (half pound) cube of C4 explosives onto the mine itself, lit the fuse, and ran. He and his squad returned to the apartment complex that I had just finished clearing.

"Get inside! Now!" Captain America yelled at us. I was currently unaware that he had placed the charge but was smart enough not to ask questions. I dropped what I was doing and dove into one of the small apartments.

A blinding, hot, white and pink flash seared the alley and shattered all of the windows. It was obvious that if the mine had not been discovered ahead of time it would have easily taken out the entire platoon.

Once again we settled in for the night, now in the newly-conquered apartment building. I stood in the corner of a bedroom, gazing out of the window from an angle that I knew to minimize exposure to snipers.

I looked over my shoulder and saw Shaft, our American MAG machine gunner from Rhode Island, praying *Erevit* (evening prayers) in the living room of the apartment. In the IDF we had a tradition of making "Tuna Soufflé" by placing squares of toilet paper into the oil of a tuna can and then igniting them. The toilet paper burned like the wick of an oil lamp and correspondingly cooked the tuna. It actually tasted a lot better than it sounded. That was the only source of light we were provided. There he sat, huddled next to a flaming can of tuna and prayed. I smiled. Hey, whatever worked.

Day 4. January 6th, 2009: Ammunition Warehouses and Greenhouses

After spending the night in a small apartment building we started our advance just before dawn. The highlight of this advance was the ultimate target: taking over a weapons depot. This weapons depot was theoretically a set of warehouses holding food and other canned supplies. Hamas, however, currently stored more rockets and rifles there than anything else.

We continued through the city and entered a group of greenhouses. Everywhere in the Gaza Strip there were greenhouses. Some of them were from the Jewish residents before they were forcefully evacuated. Most of them, however, were from a man named George Soros. George Soros was a Hungarian-American Jewish financier. He also acted as a lobbyist and philanthropist who donated billions of dollars for liberal causes. One such endeavor was the building of greenhouses for the Palestinian Arabs in the Gaza Strip. Unfortunately, however, the Palestinian Arabs failed to realize that the greenhouses only had value if they actually grew things in them. Almost every greenhouse in the Gaza Strip was in perfect working condition. But they were also full of weeds. That was something that really surprised me. The Palestinian Arabs incessantly complained of a lack of food, relying on incoming United Nations humanitarian aid. And yet they had greenhouses full of weeds standing in their backyards. One bag of seeds and half an hour of time would supply a family with fresh produce for months. But that involved work. It also involved the empowerment of the local populace, which was not something that Hamas and the other terror-mafias wanted.

Likewise, because the ground was so fertile and because once upon a time there was produce there were now onions, potatoes, and various other edibles growing randomly. Sometimes I could even find a rogue onion or potato defiantly flourishing in the gutter. These onions and potatoes provided a creative way for us soldiers to add some variety to the tuna and mini-salami sticks that we ate exclusively for the entire operation.

This greenhouse was no exception and was also full of weeds and an occasional lonely onion. My platoon entered the large greenhouse first and waited. Then the mortars began the bombardment as usual. During the operation I had discovered that the IDF apparently had no real doctrine of "Danger Close." In the American military it was an official rule that there would be no bombardment within three hundred meters of their own troops. In the Israeli military I was beginning to realize that there was no such rule. The previous day we had been in a house and the designated marksmen were taking positions near the windows. Axl and another designated marksman, Ex-Lax, were having a disagreement about the safety goggles we wore during urban warfare. Ex-Lax insisted that it was okay to take them off but Axl wasn't so sure. A few moments later one of the choppers sighted a threat of some kind in the house next to us. They fired a missile. The whole house jolted violently and all of the windows that weren't already broken shattered. The shards of glass flew to the opposite side of the room and every soldier inside the house dove to the ground. Captain America called over the radio and demanded that they cease firing, or at the very least give us some kind of forewarning.

Here in the greenhouse it wasn't much different. The mortars and missiles fell. The demolitions platoon also took down a few buildings. With every large explosion I watched flaming debris land on the transparent roof of the greenhouse just over my head. I listened to the trickling sound of small pieces of stone and concrete landing on tin roofs and the transparent greenhouse roofing. It was not unlike a momentary, passing hailstorm.

After the initial bombardment we moved forward. We entered the depot. By this time it was abandoned and most, but not all, of the weapons removed. We found a brand-new Toyota Land Cruiser valued at approximately fifty thousand dollars parked near the office. The Land Cruiser had been outfitted with a custom package, including leather seats as well as specially-designed Hamas hood ornaments and other paraphernalia. When I found the car it had already taken heavy damage from the bombing and shooting. Amazingly, despite the excessive mutilation from bullets and shrapnel, one of the tires remained inflated.

"I haven't done this since I was back in the United States!" I announced as I whipped out my commando knife and stabbed the tire. I felt a personal satisfaction from the ensuing hissing sound.

We got a good laugh out of it but I was still reminded by Captain America that this was not our goal in the operation. "The place is already full of terrorists. They don't need any more." And he was right. It was extremely important to remain professional and looting was not the objective. Still, the car had already been all but destroyed and Hamas had bought it with misappropriated humanitarian funding and given it a custom hood ornament even. So I felt no qualms of conscience.

We also found a pocket-sized Quran in the glove box. As soon as we realized what it was we returned it and it remained undisturbed. The thought did occur to me that in the past the Palestinian Arabs had been considerably less considerate with our holy sites and religious writings, usually profaning them and/or destroying them.

We were just about finished with the assignment of the day. We continued the usual pattern of entry and covering fire, taking and searching house and building after house and building. At one point we were moving along a house with a large quantity of smoke billowing out of the windows and openings. A propane tank had been inside and the mortars ignited it. Now the house was on fire and there were a few more propane tanks outside. We kept moving as quickly as possible without exposing ourselves to gunfire.

We made the depot the new logistics rendezvous. This part of the city would be our new base of operations for the next few days while we waited (as usual) for the rest of the army to advance and the politicians to... do whatever it was that politicians did. I had yet to figure that out.

Day 5. January 7th, 2009: Police Mode Vs. War Mode

We had established our position at the very front of the Israeli offensive into the Gaza Strip. We were it. We were the front line. We had advanced faster and farther than any other unit in the IDF. Such being the case we accepted a request to help the 101st Battalion of the Paratroopers. They had also continued their advance. But they had not yet cleared out all of the houses in their area of operations. So while they secured themselves also on the very front we sent a platoon to go behind them and thoroughly check the residential areas that 101 had passed through for weapons, explosives, and anything else along those lines.

That platoon was us, Platoon Six of Heavy Weapons & Recon, Battalion 890.

We began our entrance into the Palestinian Arab neighborhood. This entrance, however, was unlike all of our other offensives. All of our other advances had been in full war mode against mostly abandoned and very rich Hamas neighborhoods. The little human population we encountered consisted exclusively of a scattered collection of heavily armed terrorists sporting AK-47's, Dragonuv sniper rifles, and classic RPG's. We smashed them hard and without hesitation.

This neighborhood, however, was not a Hamas neighborhood. It was therefore not a rich neighborhood either. In the IDF we had two basic *modus operandus*. I called them "War Mode" and "Police Mode." In "War Mode" we destroyed pretty much everything and everyone. We did our best to avoid civilian casualties, and certainly did not target them. However, if "civilians" insisted on remaining in a declared war zone, especially after we had begun heavy bombardment and dropped thousands of leaflets, then there was a very real possibility that they were unfortunately going to suffer. The problem was that terrorists, contrary to popular opinion, did not walk around in uniforms and carry Hamas flags. They wore civilian clothing. This factor created a huge headache for the Rules of Engagement and was also considered a war crime according to the Fourth Geneva Convention. Under normal circumstances an individual taking a stroll in non-military clothing was a civilian. But the moment he pulled a hand grenade out of his pocket he became a terrorist and a threat. One thing that always seemed ironic to me, however, was that the moment he threw the hand grenade he immediately became unarmed. And, to my confusion, he was now considered a civilian again. This was one of the reasons why the calculations of "civilians" killed varied so much between Hamas and Israeli figures. (And, of course, the obvious fact that Hamas lied...) In the mindset of Hamas, the sixteen year-old youth that just threw a hand grenade was now currently unarmed and therefore should not be killed, especially because he was only sixteen. I personally strongly differed with that idea. I felt that any if person, even a sixteen year-old kid, threw a hand grenade at anybody else (especially me) he should be promptly and immediately shot. I could relate from personal experience that I had seen sixteen year-old teenagers kill just as well, or better, than sixty year-old men. And the teenager knew full-well what he was doing.

In "War Mode" we destroyed. We shot first and asked questions later. In "Police Mode," however, we functioned much more like an American SWAT team and did our best to capture and interrogate. We assumed that human contact was civilian until proven to be a threat.

For this assignment Captain America informed us that we were switching to "Police Mode." Apparently 101 had spotted numerous persons in the area and they were not an immediate Hamas threat. We were making entry into that neighborhood to determine just that. It was possible that they were merely civilians who for some unknown reason had decided to sit in their houses while we bombed everything around them. Or it was possible that they were actually Hamas-affiliated, or associated with one of the many other terror organizations in the Gaza Strip.

We entered the neighborhood. I placed my M4 assault rifle around a corner and covered Captain America and Afula. Afula was our radioman. He was leading the offensive with Captain America due to his ability to speak Arabic. Originally he had learned to speak both Arabic and English from the *shuks* and marketplaces of northern Israel. He later touched up his linguistic skills with military courses in interrogation and hostage negotiation.

I scanned the narrow alleyways with Shaft at my side. He worked to steady his very heavy MAG 7.62mm squad machine gun, ready to send a massive volley of bullets down a side alley if any threat made the mistake of approaching.

There we remained. The tension was high. We knew for a fact that there was human contact in the area. And, because we were in "Police Mode," the tension was even higher. "Police Mode" was much more dangerous because we waited until the human contact proved himself to be a threat before we killed him. This aspect meant that if he was a suicide bomber or had any kind of weapon he had the advantage of our hesitation. And they knew it, too.

I knelt at the corner for what seemed like an eternity. A donkey walked by. Then a rooster. Then a dog. Then a small horse. Then a group of sheep. Then a cat. Then a goat. And then, to my surprise, an entire gaggle[1] of ducks waddled by. And there, with my assault rifle ready to fire, and Shaft next to me with an enormous machine gun, I couldn't resist but comment.

"Hey, Shaft," I hissed across the alley. "What is this? Are we assaulting a petting zoo?!"

The problem was that he started laughing. We both did our best to remain as quiet as possible. It broke the tension but two Americans holding machine guns and laughing wasn't a smart idea. Major Bloodlust was in the area and gave us a warning glance, sending the obvious message that we needed to stay serious and control ourselves.

Captain America and Afula neared the entrance of one of the houses. That is, if you could call it a house. It was more like a group of large shacks thrown together somehow. Afula began to shout in Arabic. I spoke no Arabic but some words were very similar to Hebrew. I could pick up a little bit here and there. Likewise, he translated it all into Hebrew for Captain America.

"If there is anyone inside come out and surrender immediately! If you do not then you will be killed!"

Without hesitation an entire family exited the dwelling. Out came a man, his several wives, and numerous children. They were all obviously very poor and unarmed. We leveled our rifles at them but did not shoot. Afula carried on the conversation, asking basic questions such as "Do you have any weapons?" and "Is there anyone else inside?"

The answer to both questions was "No." We proceeded to tie up the men with cable ties and blindfold them. The women we didn't touch. Then we told the

men and their families to sit in a certain corner of their "yard" and we guarded them. I then proceeded to enter to "house" and check for weapons.

[1 While watching the ducks go by, I was unable to determine what the proper collective term was for a group of ducks. After careful research, I discovered that "gaggle" was incorrect and the word is used exclusively for geese. A variety of words may be used for ducks depending on whether the ducks are in water, on land, or in flight. The terms include, "flock", "team", "paddling", and "waddling". Although this information is completely irrelevant, that sad truth is that I was actually concerned about this grammatical technicality during a military operation in the Gaza Strip.]

These people had no connection to Hamas. Therefore they were unarmed and very, very poor. I went through the house searching everywhere for weapons, doing my best not to damage what little they had.

We continued on to the next residences, leaving soldiers to guard the first family. Afula again called out in Arabic, and again a similar-looking family exited. Again they were poor and unarmed.

It was the same story more or less, but there was a little twist to the conversation. This time there was still one person inside the residence, but he was "too sick" to exit. Afula told the father that if he did not come out he would be killed. The father of the family protested, saying in Arabic (that I actually understood) that he was mentally ill and therefore simply incapable of exiting. We were unsure of what to do. The only reasonable solution it seemed was to proceed with caution. Maybe there was someone legitimately unable to exit the shack. Maybe it was a trap and there was someone sitting there waiting for me to round the corner holding a machine gun, grenade, or an RPG. I moved forward and "opened the corner," as we called it in Hebrew, finger on the trigger and ready for anything.

I would never forget what I saw in there. I can't even begin to properly to describe what was in that shed. Neither do I really want to. I saw what bore some resemblance of a human being. But his mental faculties were so low that he was living like an animal... worse than an animal. He was filthy, covered in his own urine, feces, and some sort of wet mush that he apparently considered "food."

I looked over my shoulder to Sergeant Obama.

"What is this place? Where are we?"

Then he explained. This neighborhood was incredibly poor. It also consisted largely of Bedouin Arabs. It was basically a colony of sorts of the extremely poor, the physically ill, and the mentally disabled. Most of them were inbred even, the result of incestuous polygamy. They were simply financially, physically, or mentally incapable of fleeing our assault and bombardment. So there they sat, with mortars and bombs falling all around them, waiting their fate.

Hamas, the great "Martyrs of Freedom," "Warriors of the People," had left them there to die. These people were too poor and/or sick to be of any use to them.

At one point one of our soldiers, Danny-Boy, peered out the window and checked for threats from the outside. Almost immediately a bullet slammed into the wall just next to his head. But it wasn't a terrorist threat. It was one of our own snipers. He was not part of our battalion and had been both confused as to our location as well as a bit trigger-happy. The saddest part of Operation: Cast Lead was that we ended up killing more of our own soldiers with friendly fire than even Hamas did.

After checking the house I sat on the "porch" and guarded the family. One of the men was sick with a pretty bad cold. He was tied up and blindfolded, just to be on the safe side. But his nose was dirty. Sergeant Obama asked me if I still had my toilet paper (an obvious necessity in the army). He then gave one of the women a strip of tissue and permission to briefly clean his nose.

Another soldier, however, wasn't as sympathetic. We had given him the nickname "Commander Darwin" due to his obvious stupidity and because he was quite clearly the missing link of Darwinian evolution. Commander Darwin first complained that we were in "Police Mode" rather than "War Mode." Captain America harshly rebuked him for that comment. He later began an argument with a half-crazy old woman. She was rambling on an on, something about Allah protecting them and so forth. I ignored her but Commander Darwin began a theological debate with her. Sergeant Obama and I both grew angry. Sergeant Obama, the superior officer to both of us, told him in no uncertain terms to shut his mouth.

I agreed completely with Sergeant Obama. I had absolutely no problem killing terrorists. And I would continue to shoot them and blow them up and utterly destroy their headquarters and mansions at every opportunity and not think twice about it. These people, however, were *not* my enemy. I didn't think they particularly liked me, but so what? They were incapable in all facets of doing anything negative to me or the Jewish people. So just leave them alone.

Axl claimed later that he saw Commander Darwin secretly, intentionally, and unnecessarily damage their property while searching for weapons. Axl later made a comment about it to me and the IDF doctor. The military doctor was enraged and swore that he would have Commander Darwin investigated and put in jail.

His fate had yet to be determined.[1]

It was with great embarrassment that I related the account of Commander Darwin. But I wrote it for two reasons. First, I wanted my story to be as accurate as possible. True history is the real story, not just the parts we want to remember. Also there was a very serious moral to be learned from his actions. Blind hate was the reason why there was no peace for the Jewish people. People hated us blindly. But if we responded to blind hate with more blind hate, it became a vicious circle and ultimately more people died. I hated Hamas. I hated terrorism. I did not and do not hate the Palestinian Arabs who had neither the capability nor the intention of carrying out violence against the Jewish people and who likewise suffered from the reign of their terror-mafias.

After a few hours we untied the men and left. I looked at the faces of the men, curious to see how they were responding to being tied up and blindfolded for several hours. To my surprise they were laughing about it. They would probably forever tell their friends and family about the day they "survived the Israeli assault," and sat tied up for several hours. Just as I told my stories I am sure that long after they were telling their stories. Maybe there was even a blog somewhere in Arabic on the internet... or a book.

As we were leaving one of the wives who did not suffer from any mental handicaps admitted to us that they were suffering from Hamas as well. My initial thought was that she was simply trying to patronize us, lying to us in order to gain favor. But I thought twice about that judgment as I returned to the previously conquered Hamas mansion just down the street complete with computers, plasma screen televisions, and a greenhouse full of weeds.

No, I didn't think she was lying. She knew who the real enemy was. And it wasn't me.

[1 While insufficient evidence was provided to put him in military jail for that particular offense, Major Bloodlust and Captain America had seen and heard enough that they officially got fed up with him. He was demoted and deemed unworthy to continue service with the *Mesayat* Heavy Weapon & Recon Company. He was moved to a different company. It was their loss and our gain. Two other soldiers were later caught trying to steal cheap jewelry from a destroyed Hamas house. The jewelry was confiscated and they were sentenced to jail for thirty days.]

Day Six. January 8th, 2009: Inner Turmoil

We stayed in our Hamas mansion at the very front of the advance. I soon discovered that waiting in the same place was more dangerous than advancing. By sitting in the same house it became obvious to Hamas where we were located. And although we had established defensive positions it drained us physically and mentally to stare at the same empty alley or neighborhood. The problem was that we knew the moment we let down our guard someone would come strolling down the road with a suicide belt of explosives or an RPG. But we also had to guard ourselves against shooting recklessly and possibly hitting our own troops.

We continued searching Hamas houses. We found uniforms, handguns, AK-47's, RPG's, explosives, and a collection of similar items. At one point Captain America found a safe. He placed C4 explosives on the safe to detonate it and open it. We were the missile platoon, however, and *not* the explosives platoon. He used just a tad bit too much.

He succeeded in opening the safe but blew up everything inside as well. We watched thousands of dollars, pounds, francs, shekels, dinars, and several other currencies fly around the room and burn.

Oops...

I personally got a kick out of my two discoveries. I found the popular "Grand Theft Auto" video game next to a computer. This video game, however, had been edited by Moslem hackers and was now "Grand Theft Auto: Gaza City," complete with all street signs converted to Arabic and the characters themselves made to look more Arab.

We also found an official Hamas "end-of-training" t-shirt, very similar to the t-shirts we received in the IDF at the end of our advanced training. I was tempted to take the shirt and write on it, "I went to war in the Gaza Strip and all I got was this lousy t-shirt!"

On a more serious note we received bad news about one of the *Maslul* (on-the-job training) platoons of our battalion. This was Rambo's company. They had been clearing out houses. Their platoon-commanding lieutenant, Aharon Karov, was one of the best friends of our platoon-commander, Captain America. He had been storming a Hamas house. He climbed the stairs cautiously. His head was slightly above the level of the second floor. A booby trap exploded and sent shrapnel into his mouth and through part of his brain. He survived, but was obviously in critical condition.

229

The saddest thing about this story was that Lieutenant Karov had just gotten married a week before. We had just received orders that we were preparing to go into the Gaza Strip in a ground operation. He had already planned his wedding and barely received half a day away from the base. He literally got married and returned the same day just before we went into the Gaza Strip.

After the war I was unsure of his current condition. I had heard that he was able to recognize his wife and family and squeeze when the doctor said squeeze, etc. He was currently unable to communicate. But that might have been because of all the tubes in his mouth and other medical paraphernalia[1]

These were the questions that every soldier thought about after the war. Why not me? Why him? Of the few casualties in Operation: Cast Lead, and of all the soldiers, why him? Why the religious Jew, the endeavoring and aspiring lieutenant, the newlywed? Why not the soldier without a family? Why not the soldier who was corrupt and only there because of the mandatory draft?

This was the way we thought as humans. This was also the way Iyov (Job) was thinking and presented the exact same question first to his friends and later HaShem Himself after, in a single moment, he lost his entire family and all his possessions. "Why me? It's not fair."

HaShem's only real answer to Iyov was that He had a plan. He had created the world and knew what He was doing.

I was sure that rabbis had multitudes of comments on the matter. I, however, was not a rabbi. I was merely a soldier. I did my best not to think about it too much. All I could do was mention his name in my *davening* (prayers) and continue my part in the operation. The rabbis would continue to fight to discover the mysteries of the universe. I would meanwhile continue to fight the terrorists down the street... then ask the rabbis for their conclusions afterwards.

[1] He still had a long road to recovery, but the doctors were amazed at his progress. He was even in good enough condition to attend the end-of-training ceremony for his troops a few months later, which included my American friend, Rambo. Eventually he had practically a complete recovery, which has been described as nothing short of miraculous.]

Day 7. January 9th, 2009: Our Secret Weapon

Today was a very happy day for me. I finally got my toothbrush! We had been told to place all toothbrushes and similar items that we did not absolutely need for the initial assault into a bag. The bag would then be delivered to us on the morning of the second day after the initial entry. And silly me, I actually believed that would happen.

Somewhere along the line our logistics team misplaced the bag. So this whole time I had been without any toothbrush or deodorant of any kind. In my mind it was our new secret weapon against Hamas: eating tuna for a week with no toothbrush in sight. Our breath and body odor alone would kill them. Finally, after a week of not being able to brush our teeth, our logistics personnel sent us all new toothbrushes and toothpaste. I didn't know who donated them but I wanted to truly thank them from the very bottom of my heart. (And for all the other donations, by the way.)[1] I brushed my teeth... twice. I reveled and delighted in the wonderful, minty freshness.[2]

We were still in that same house... waiting. There was some kind of debate amongst the generals as well. Some were in favor of pushing south and proceeding all the way to [-------]. Others preferred that we exit and then reenter and conquer [-------], an area known for weapons storage [*Censored for security*]. We waited for our orders.

The first lieutenant of the Heavy Weapons & Recon Company, Captain Crunch, informed us of another small assignment. There was an additional neighborhood that needed to be searched. This neighborhood was abandoned but was not a Hamas neighborhood. It was a Fatah (PLO) area.

Captain Crunch and Sergeant Obama led the squad, checking the neighborhood for weapons. As the lead designated marksman if there was a locked door I would shoot it out. (It worked better in the movies). Even after shooting the lock the door wouldn't always open. In such circumstances we would simply blow down the door with a variety of explosive devices.

We searched numerous small houses. These Fatah members apparently suffered financially for opposing Hamas and were living in small one room shacks compared to the Hamas mansions. It was a unique feeling walking into a small house and seeing a huge photo of Yasir Arafat framed on the wall. We were in a completely different world. But the strangest thing of all was that

[1 We received a flood of generous donations, for all of which we were greatly appreciative. I had been asked what the best thing to donate to soldiers was. I have a few comments and recommendations for those who wish to extend their generosity to IDF soldiers during a combat operation.

We received massive quantities of Israeli chocolate. As delicious as this was, it got to the point of becoming a staple of our diet, combined with tuna and dried kosher sausages. Healthier alternatives, such as energy bars, granola bars, nuts, dried fruit, etc., might be better in the long run. Additionally, it was difficult to get anything to drink besides water, although a certain flavored soda water corporation donated a large amount of their drink products. Sport drinks, iced tea, and maybe even cola products would be ideal.

A combat operation is essentially a long-term and dangerous camping trip. Related supplies such as hand sanitizer and baby wipes are always in high demand. Clean socks, gloves, and other clothing and gear for warmth are also welcome, assuming the operation is carried out in the winter time. Also, specialized combat boots and weapon accessories, particularly forward hand grips, are always in demand.

I personally always enjoyed a brief personal message from the donors. Even a hand-written post-it note went a long way. In one package of donations I received a letter from a Hebrew school student named Ted B. By the time I received the donations it was almost a year later (a fact I would have preferred to have known *before* I ate the chocolate.) To his surprise I wrote him back and we exchanged correspondence several times after that.

And, of course, I can't speak highly enough of Friends of the IDF. This is an excellent organization that does indeed distribute donations, both financial and otherwise, to places where it really counts. All throughout my service on practically every military base I saw fully-equipped gyms and soldier lounges proudly displaying the FIDF logo. And as a *chayal boded,* or lone soldier, I personally received many gifts and benefits from the organization. I am the biggest skeptic of non-profit organizations because I always worry where the money goes to. I can say from personal experience that with Friends of the IDF the soldiers *do* receive the benefits... and a lot of them. And this is particularly true for lone soldiers such as myself.

Thank you again for your support.]

[2 I hope everyone realizes the kind of sacrifices I was making and the hardships I faced for the Jewish people.]

after I exited the small house and checked the roof I could see the smokestacks from a factory in the nearby Israeli port city of Ashkelon.

Home was so close, and yet it never felt so far away.

Day 8. January 10th, 2009: A Sad Decision

We were officially sick and tired of waiting in that same house. The generals and/or politicians needed to make up their minds on what they wanted to do.

This night, for some strange reason, we were ordered to leave the house for one night only and guard the logistics rendezvous of Battalion 101. I never really did understand why we were sent. And it was very cold. It reminded me of our first night in the Gaza Strip, but not quite as severe.

Being in the Gaza Strip with little to no contact to the outside world we really had no idea what was going on in the rest of civilization. What we did know was that the world was angry with us. That was a big shocker. We did *not* know, however, that almost[1] the entire country of Israel and especially the Jewish communities outside of Israel were behind us and supported us. Even the more left wing political groups that normally disapproved of military operations in the Gaza Strip were in favor. The question in Israel was not so much "Should we?" as it was "How should we?" Or, more specifically, "How much?" and "How far?"

[1] I found out later that about this time Axl's girlfriend, M'SLF, had an interesting encounter. (The origin of the nickname is another story entirely). She walked into a bar/restaurant and began to watch the news of the operation on the large flat-screen television. There was an extreme left-wing Israeli girl sitting on the bar stool next to her and she started shaking her head. When M'SLF asked what was wrong the girl replied, "I hope that every single Israeli soldier dies or gets captured and tortured."

"Excuse me," M'SLF retorted, obviously unhappy with this comment, "But my boyfriend and one of my closest friends (i.e., yours truly) are down there."

Without even missing a beat the girl looked M'SLF in the eyes and responded, "Well then, I hope that your boyfriend and close friend die!"

And without further ceremony M'SLF took a swing and punched her in the face, knocking her off of her bar stool and drawing blood. M'SLF then fled the scene before the police arrived. As M'SLF later commented, "Sometimes you've just gotta punch a loudmouth..." All glory and respect to M'SLF, Axl's girlfriend. This was the kind of support that our troops needed.]

We did hear, however, that Hezbollah fired missiles at northern Israel from Lebanon. We all groaned when we heard this news. I had always been worried about that. The last thing I wanted was a war on two fronts. The Paratroopers especially were the most mobile of all the military units. That meant that if we survived the Gaza Strip we would be immediately sent to Lebanon, or at least, to the northern border. We later heard that Hezbollah vehemently denied responsibility for the missile attacks and it didn't happen again. Supposedly it was a different Palestinian Arab group trying to get the north involved. But Hezbollah didn't like that idea at all. They probably saw what we were doing in the Gaza Strip and thought twice about bringing the "Zionist War Machine" back into southern Lebanon. I hoped so. That was kind of the idea.

We also heard rumors about our mortar platoon, Platoon Seven. Hamas had set up two missile and mortar positions on the roof of a United Nations school and forced the civilians, mostly children, to remain inside. With at least thirty-five children and other civilians beneath Hamas terrorists began a mortar bombardment. They also commenced firing the Russian-made "Grad" missiles towards Ashkelon, Ashdod, and my apartment.

So what could we do in that situation? My friends sat in their APC's (Armored Personnel Carriers) and aimed their *Keshet*-system heavy mortars. They had the enemy mortar and missile launchers and their crews targeted. They knew that if they pushed that button they would probably kill dozens of Palestinian Arab children. But they also knew that if they did *not* push that button there was a good chance that they would kill dozens of our children, not to mention the mortars that were an immediate threat to the soldiers' lives. According to the Fourth Geneva Convention by forcing civilians to remain in the area the Hamas terrorists had committed a very grave war crime. Additionally, the Fourth Geneva Convention specifically states that protected areas such as schools and hospitals lose their "protected status" if they are being used for the purpose of an armed conflict. So what did they do?

They pushed the button.

The mortar and missile crews were immediately destroyed, the threat to Israeli civilians eliminated, and the lives of dozens of Palestinian Arabs, many of which were children, extinguished in a single moment. It is still considered an "international incident" of great debate to this day.

It brought to mind a quote by Golda Meir, former Prime Minister of Israel:

"There will be peace in the Middle East when the Arabs love their own children more than they hate ours."

I have the following message to say to Hamas or anyone that is upset with IDF military operations: Contrary to popular opinion we do *not* enjoy killing children. Stop shooting missiles and firing mortars from schools, hospitals, and mosques. (In fact, how about you stop shooting them completely.) It wasn't a difficult concept. But if they were to do that, then Hamas wouldn't have the opportunity to make the Israel Defense Force look bad.[1]

Were the lives of their wives and children worth bad publicity for the Israeli military? Only they could answer that question. But so far in my military experience the answer had been a repeated and deplorable "Yes."

[1] Even now I have never been able to get the complete story on what happened there. The account mentioned here was based on the accounts that I heard from other platoons of ground forces. Some sources said the school itself was bombed, some said it was a building next to the school. There was also a disagreement as to which platoon actually did the bombing. Originally I heard that it was our Platoon Seven, but later someone swore profusely it was a Givati platoon. There was definitely terrorist activity involved, even the Hamas sources admitted that. The media reported that a large number of terrorist bodies were found in the rubble. The Goldstone report was hesitant to declare that the terrorist threat legitimized the bombing of the school. Israel said "Yes," Hamas said "No." The Fourth Geneva Convention could be quoted as saying in Article 28,

"The presence of a protected person (civilian) may not be used to render certain points or areas immune from military operations,"

And Article 51.7 stated,

"The presence or movements of the civilian population or individual civilians shall not be used to render certain points or areas immune from military operations, in particular in attempts to shield military objectives from attacks or to shield, favor, or impede military operation."

The point is this: If there was a single terrorist in that school then Hamas had committed an official war crime against humanity and the Israeli government was under no legal obligation to spare the lives of the civilians, once again contrary to popular opinion. Launching a mortar attack against that school, as horrific and tragic as it was, was both necessary and permissible according to international law and *not* a war crime. The only war crime committed here was by Hamas.]

Day 9. January 11th, 2009: A Culinary Curse

Finally we received our orders. We were to continue farther south to Jabaliyah, very close to Gaza City itself.

We prepared to leave that evening. At about five in the evening we started to move. We proceeded for about five minutes, and then we were told to return to that same lousy house. The mission had been postponed. I was not sure what the reason was. We were also having issues with a suicide bomber squad led by a certain Hamas woman. I bestowed upon her the moniker of "Delilah." Delilah headed a suicide bomber and RPG squad that irritated us the entire operation. They would move, intel and/or recon would spot them, and then they would disappear.

We returned to the house and waited, keeping a careful eye out for Delilah or one of her crew.

Meanwhile, we came up with a new culinary discovery. Being tired of tuna, Shaft, Axl, and I actually *requested* a few cans of Loof in our next logistic drop. What was Loof? It was basically kosher corned beef in a can. If there was a kosher version of Spam, it would be Loof. I was not sure who the man was that brought the curse of Spam upon the non-Jewish world. But someone apparently thought that the Jewish people, particularly the Israelis, should not be exempt from this affliction. They made Loof as a kosher substitute, using kosher beef instead of pork. Loof was so disgusting that there had actually been efforts and even movements to ban it from the IDF. I had seen it used as a punishment as well, forcing a non-complying soldier to eat an entire can in a short period of time. Somehow, however, it managed to survive the negative onslaught, and it was still an important part of IDF field supplies.

I remember on one occasion back in training I got a hold of a few extra cans and mailed them to my friends in the United States. Not being able to read the Hebrew very well they were unsure of what it was. They opened it and decided it was dog food. Their terrier loved it.

Our American (and Canadian) trio had discovered a way to make it palpable. We chopped the Loof first into very small cubes. We mixed it with onions (found growing in the gutter) and various spices. We then cooked it on a propane burner with a touch of corn oil and placed it into a roll. It actually wasn't too bad. Either that, or we were just that sick of tuna and mini-salami sticks.

We dubbed our new sandwich "The Meaty Axl."

Day 10. January 12th, 2009: Attack Pigeons

We received orders to recommence our mission and to leave the house. Once again, however, the mission was postponed. We advanced only slightly and moved into a beach-side resort house. The house itself was beautiful but rather uncomfortable. It was still under construction and therefore lacked furniture.

A strange feature of this house was pigeons. But they were not just any pigeons. I had never encountered birds like these. They were like giant Hamas pigeons from hell, as stupid as that sounds. These pigeons were huge and they weren't afraid of anything. They would waddle up to us and become openly irritated for "invading their space." They would begin pecking at our feet, expressing their annoyance. They wouldn't leave me alone unless I pushed them away with my foot. Then they would fly around the corner of the building for exactly thirty seconds and then return, twice as many of them as before, and actually attack us. I had never seen anything like it in my life. It was so unusual we even made videos of it.

In this house we met up with Platoon Five, the Recon Platoon. I soon found my good friends, Wee-Man from South Africa and Cueball from Connecticut, USA. As soldiers always do we began swapping stories.

Not all the stories and rumors heard in the army were accurate or truthful. At one point I even heard a claim that one of our best special forces units had located and rescued the previously kidnapped soldier, Gilad Shalit. I immediately discredited this rumor as false, as it obviously was.

I also heard a report about an almost successful attempt by Hamas to kidnap another one of our soldiers, but I was never able to get enough details to verify the validity of this rumor.

Wee-Man and Cueball did relate a confirmed story involving a true miracle. The Recon Platoon had been advancing to another position. Because they were reconnaissance they were often, but not always, much farther forward than most other platoons. In this particular case they had moved so far ahead that the tanks had not yet realized their presence. The tanks received the wrong coordinates of a Hamas squad, saw the Recon Platoon, and fired a shell at them. The shell landed in the sand at the feet of a Russian-Israeli commander. The sand, however, apparently had not been dense enough to detonate the shell. It skidded "harmlessly" to a halt about a meter away from him. He stood there haplessly, staring in shock at the unexploded tank shell.

Another battalion of the Paratroopers wasn't so lucky. Their first lieutenant had led a platoon into a house and conquered it. Similarly, the tanks had been unaware of their incursion and had received distorted coordinates of Hamas activity. To make it worse the first lieutenant briefly took off his helmet, presumably to adjust the straps. The tanks put a shell into the house through the window. This shell, however, did explode. He was killed instantaneously.[1]

Cueball and Weeman had another story for me. They were making an urban assault when one of the designated marksmen of Platoon Five spotted a figure in the window of a neighboring house. He called it in. The person was dressed in a civilian sweater, standing near the window, and taking notes on a notepad. It was obvious that he was spying for Hamas against the Israeli advance. The designated marksman received permission to fire. He misjudged the range, however, and barely missed, hitting just above his head. It turned out that the figure was the soldier of another battalion entirely. While stationed in the Hamas house he had become cold, put on a civilian sweater, taken off his helmet, stood next to the window, and began making notes of… nobody knew what. It was not a very smart thing to do. And he almost paid for it with his life.

The corresponding question had been posed to me many times: "Why was there so much friendly fire?" There were three basic reasons friendly fire occurred.

First of all, there was something called "The Fog of War." When everything was literally exploding around us the human body entered into a state of shock that made proper and accurate communication very difficult. The deafening noise didn't help either. An entire group of people trying to function in this state of shock, noise, and confusion was highly problematic. One of the most important goals of military training was to reduce this shock to a minimum and to teach soldiers to operate automatically and according to instincts. While training helped dramatically it did not totally eliminate this shock factor.

Another problem was a lack of cohesion as it was referred to in Hebrew, with the differing units and battalions. Within Paratroopers 890, especially the *Mesayat* Heavy Weapons & Recon Company, I usually knew exactly who was

[1] It was later reported that the father of the deceased lieutenant called up the responsible tank crew over the radio. He informed the crew that he did not hold any hatred to them for the accident. He encouraged them to continue the fight as soldiers of Israel and protectors of the Jewish people. I cannot imagine what it must be like for any father to do this.]

going where and doing what without even thinking about it. I knew from months, even years, of training and experience who was going to do what, where, why, how, etc. Additionally, I was familiar with the traits of my fellow soldiers and how they operated on a personal level. For example, I already knew if a certain soldier advanced slower or faster, if a certain soldier was reckless or cautious, etc. We did not, however, necessarily have the same knowledge as to what other units (such as the tanks) were going to do. Likewise, they did not necessarily know how we moved and operated. This fact was a recipe for confusion.

And then we must consider that people sometimes just did stupid things either from shock or some other unknown reason. While stupidity to this level was rare all it took was one person not using their brain for a few seconds to take out an entire platoon.

If there was one definite mistake of Operation: Cast Lead it was the amount of friendly fire. As aforementioned it was very, very unfortunate that many of the casualties were from friendly fire rather than Hamas reprisal.

Day 11. January 13th, 2009: The Lethal Landlord

Now we made our push forward. Our ultimate target was the city of Jabaliyah, just outside of Gaza City itself.

The assault was massive. We moved past a group of depots and warehouses. We then began to clear out a tall six or seven story apartment building. We wanted the *retik* (heavy fire crew) of the *Maslul* (on-the-job training) company to set up on the higher levels and cover our advance with their .50 caliber machine guns and their MK-19 automatic grenade launchers.

Platoon Six and Platoon Eight were in the front, as usual. I worked with my partner, Sergeant Obama, with Axl and Shaft backing me up from behind.

It was amazing to watch. One thing in particular that impressed me was the tracer rounds. The heavy machine guns had a red tracer round every so many bullets so that the gunner knew how many rounds he had shot and how many he had remaining. The red tracers looked like lasers. When the *retik* commenced firing multiple machine guns at once it was like something from a science-fiction movie.

I was surprised when we entered the neighborhood. I had thought the Hamas houses before were affluent, but this was ridiculous. In all of my urban warfare training I had prepared for cheap cinder block housing and shacks. These houses weren't merely mansions. They were palaces. I had been trained to move from dumpsters to piles of debris. In reality I was ducking from one enormous Greek-style pillar to the next, and then charging through a beautiful rose garden. One of them even had a swimming pool in his back yard! The interior was even more elaborate, with impressive marble floors, chandeliers, and even gold paneling in the bathrooms. My father's wife's mansion in Orange County, California, couldn't even compare to these houses. And I was in the middle of the Gaza Strip! It soon became quite apparent to me where all that humanitarian funding went. Half of it went to missiles, RPG's, AK-47's, and other weapons. The other half apparently went to fund the ever-so-essential interior decoration of the "suffering" Hamas Palestinian Arabs.

I recalled for a brief moment the non-Hamas Palestinian Arabs that I had encountered and their simple residences, as well as the mentally handicapped individual "living" in the shed. If only the world really knew…

But there was no time for that now. I was in the middle of a firefight. Hamas attempted to offer a strong resistance. They had already tossed a hand grenade at our *Palchod* (Forward Rifleman) Company and had lightly to moderately wounded a few of our soldiers. I thought for a second about my friend in the *Palchod* Forward Riflemen, Lunchbox from Philadelphia, and wondered how he was doing and if he was okay.

I continued to scan the windows and doors of the neighboring mansions for terrorists. Axl and I put random, well-placed bullets into the windows while Shaft used his 7.62mm MAG machine gun and strafed entire floors. We even saw several terrorists in the manor next door. We fired. We were unsure of the outcome.

We did scare most, if not all, of the terrorists out of the mansions and they made a hasty retreat down the street in order to regroup. It was a bad plan. The moment they left the "safety" of the houses the Apache Gunship helicopters began to mow them down with their nose-mounted Vulcan cannons. Those that survived the choppers fared no better. Our Platoon Seven commenced firing their highly-accurate *Keshet* mortar system into the narrow street. The explosions destroyed everything and everyone. It wasn't a pretty scene.

We had effectively set up an urban death trap. The Hamas operatives resisting us had two choices. They could remain in the houses and be shot by me or blown up by our hand grenades and rocket launchers. Or they could attempt to flee and face death from above via helicopters and/or mortars. It was quite a dilemma with no positive outcome. In that night alone we confirmed over thirty kills.

It was near dawn. We had been advancing and fighting all night. The final step of our mission was to clear out another six story apartment building. We would be spending the next day or two there, setting up both SPIKE missile positions as well as recon posts.

Because we didn't want Hamas initially to discover we were there we went in quietly and without any shooting. Previously we had entered every house with a coordinated pattern of shooting, grenade throwing, and covering fire from other platoons. With this apartment building we entered "dry," as they called it in Hebrew. This term meant we did not throw any grenades or shoot, but entered slowly, quietly, and cautiously, ready to shoot only if a threat was identified.

We entered the first floor silently and carefully. It was dark, but the room was full of many identical objects. I peered through my night vision scope but still couldn't identify them. I cautiously walked over, hoping that they weren't what I thought they were.

They were.

"Um… Lieutenant," I hissed to Captain America. "Did you see--"

"Yes, I saw them," he responded. "I know."

About half of the bottom floor of this apartment building was covered by over one hundred and fifty large propane tanks. I know because I counted them all. Each propane tank was of the industrial type, like those seen on the back of forklifts and about twice the size of those commonly used for motor homes in the United States.

It was not a Hamas trap. The landlord of this apartment building was simply an idiot who saw no problem in storing massive quantities of propane in a residential building.

If we had tossed a grenade in that apartment building or even started shooting like we had been doing all night about half of the Gaza Strip would have seen and heard us disappear in a gigantic mushroom of fire. Beyond doubt our entire platoon, maybe even the entire company, would have been killed.

Day 12. January 14th, 2009: New Boots

The sun rose and we were stationed in the six-story apartment building. I sat there on the third floor next to our SPIKE missile launcher, waiting for orders to start letting the missiles fly. There had been a disagreement between myself and Sergeant Obama over the placement of the launcher. Safety guidelines strongly discouraged launching a missile inside a room as small as the bedroom where I was located. The fiery back blast from the missile needed about five meters (eighteen feet) to spread out or else the shooter (yours truly) would be severely burned. Sergeant Obama swore that the bedroom of three meters (ten feet) was big enough. I disagreed but hoped he was right.

At some point one of my fellow soldiers replaced me at the missile launcher so that I could run to the "restroom." Unfortunately we once again had no running water. The massive D9 bulldozers had torn up all of the plumbing in the area while destroying Hamas mines and tunnels. So I had scrounged up various necessary resources, including toilet paper and a special bag designed for such a purpose. I began wandering around the apartment building in an attempt to find some facsimile of privacy in a room without any soldiers. Finally I found a small living room in a corner of the apartment building.

It wasn't long until I realized there were three problems. First off, the reason the living room was not occupied was because a handful of tanks sat just outside the window. Also, the positioning of the windows themselves provided too much exposure to the unconquered portion of the Gaza Strip. The third problem was that the aforementioned Hamas squads somehow magically knew to attack us at the worst possible time for me.

Soon after the sniper bullets started ricocheting off of the tanks. The tanks responded with an immediate and heavy bombardment. An RPG team accordingly fired off a rocket half-wildly in the general direction of the tanks just outside the living room windows.

And there I was... "busy."

Looking back on it I couldn't believe I didn't evacuate the living room. For some idiotic reason I simply stayed there and hoped for the best.

Later I was back at the missile launcher and the RPG team returned. They fired another one. This one came much closer to hitting their target. Fortunately they miscalculated the range, and the RPG dropped just short of the apartment building itself. It exploded mere meters away from the building, missing both me on the third floor as well as the one hundred and fifty propane tanks on the bottom floor. I almost fell from the force of the blast as it made its impact against the walls and windows of the building.

I was on a personal mission to find myself a pair of shoes. At the beginning of the operation my boots had been badly torn and damaged just from all the foot travel. I was beginning to have a serious problem with water and sand getting into my boots during marches or in the middle of combat, which obviously wasn't a good thing. In every house we cleared I searched for a pair of boots of some kind. We stumbled upon a large supply of Hamas military-style uniforms complete with combat boots, but they were all too small. So my next hope was that the following Hamas operatives we killed would have large feet like me. Fortunately, however, there was no need and our logistics sergeant *finally* got me my new IDF boots after over a week of requesting them. But, to be honest, I was pleasantly surprised that I received them at all.

Day 13. January 15th, 2009: Wakif!

We had already conquered Jabaliyah and were in sight of what I believed to be Gaza University. We had arrived at the border of Gaza City itself. We left the six-story apartment building and set up briefly in one of the large mansions we had conquered a few days previously. The mansion had likewise been turned into an IDF field hospital for our battalion.

If anybody benefited from the war in the Gaza Strip it was definitely their animals. After all the abandonment, bombardment, as well as troop movements (without always closing the doors and gates behind us) practically all Palestinian Arab livestock roamed happily and freely. It was a sight to behold. Beautiful Arabian stallions munched contentedly on grass next to Israeli tanks. Cows waddled by basking in self-importance. And herds of sheep danced down the alleys.

Having only eaten Loof and tuna for weeks I was tempted to put into practice what I had learned watching an observant Jewish friend of mine slaughter a sheep and accordingly set up my own shwarma pit right there in the backyard of this Hamas mansion. My officers, however, were far less enthusiastic about the idea than I was.

Night fell and we prepared to move. Once again, however, the mission was postponed. Again, I was unsure of the reason. They didn't tell me such things. But they did tell one thing: Delilah and her suicide bomber squad were back.

I went on a midnight patrol with Sergeant Obama to secure the perimeter. We were playing cat and mouse with suicide bombers. We moved swiftly and silently from point to point, keeping a constant eye and watching through night vision gun scopes and goggles. We searched for an hour and found nothing. We returned to the residence.

About an hour later Falcon, our Russian-Israeli designated marksman, heard a scuffling sound just outside the front door of the house and saw a black figure dart past the window. He was on watch at the time at a window about a meter away from the door. He improved his position and called out to the figure.

"*Mizeh?!* Who is it?!" He shouted first in Hebrew, to be sure that he didn't shoot one of our own soldiers. Just the night before the reservists had accidentally opened fire on the colonel's entourage and wounded several soldiers due to poor communication and a lack of precaution.

There was no answer.

Falcon leveled his gun and continued scanning through the night vision scope, attempting to locate his target.

"*Wakif! Wakif!*" He called in Arabic with a thick Russian accent.[1] "*Wakif*" was an Arabic term for "Stop" and the beginning of a phrase we used in the IDF that meant "Stop! Surrender and put up your hands!" Any soldier that heard "*Wakif*" knew he better make sure the other soldier was aware of his true identity because he was probably just seconds away from getting shot.

And then, as if to answer his Arabic command, Falcon heard the unmistakable "B-a-a-a-h!" of a lost sheep, large and black.

Delilah never showed up. At least, I never saw her. But a few more false alarms like this and she wouldn't even need to bother coming to the house to blow herself up.

[1 There are differing versions of this account, one in which Falcon called out in Arabic before the sheep identified itself, and one in which he did not. I did not consider this detail significant enough to warrant extensive research on the matter and related the above version. I included the footnote to maintain as high of a standard of accuracy as possible.]

Day 14. January 16th, 2009: Stumbling Upon a Tunnel

Tonight we actually carried out the previously mentioned mission to improve our position just outside of Gaza City.

We set up the *retik* (heavy fire crew) once again in a tall apartment building. Most of the platoons were to lead the assault from the beach. We advanced along the shore and kept our heads down, ducking behind a relatively high sand embankment. As the lead designated marksman I crawled through the sand up to a chunk of concrete rubble and took a position. I fired at a nearby group of houses, scanning for enemy contacts in the windows and doorways. The mission was basically a beach-head version of the attack on Day 11. Unlike Day 11, however, we advanced farther into Gaza itself and prepared for a series of day-time operations.

We advanced along the beach. We used a stair-stepping pattern, called bounding in the US military, in which one or two soldiers advanced while the remaining soldiers provided covering fire. I was taking cover behind a chunk of concrete on the beach. It was my turn according to the pattern to advance. I called it out and charged forward.

The enemy began mortaring the beach. A small mortar landed behind the chunks of rubble exactly where I had been a mere few seconds earlier. Axl later described the scene and related that he saw a large cloud of smoke, sand, and debris rise into the air. He thought for sure that I had been blown to pieces. He wasn't the only one. An officer got on the radio and ordered a medic to be sent in to see if anything was left of me.

Fortunately for me, I had gotten out of there only a few seconds before. I continued to charge down the beach and reached a forward position of safety. Axl and the officer then saw me to their relief and called back the medic.[1]

[1 The beach assault was so chaotic with all the shooting and bombing that I actually had no idea that this had happened and that I had such a close call at all until Axl mentioned it about a month later. Also, I suspect that I "blacked-out." I discovered later that one of the side-effects of being in an intense combat situation was that the mind would dissociate from reality and act on instinct. It was apparently not uncommon for military personnel to "black out" during a combat experience and accordingly have little to no more memory of the events that transpired.]

We continued moving forward and I tripped on an invisible wire. My initial thought was that it was fishing line attached to a booby trap. Sergeant Obama explained, however, that it was fiber-optic wiring from all the rockets and missiles that the gunship helicopters had been launching. After the missile was fired there was a yarn-like ball of fiber-optic wiring inside the missile casing that unraveled. This wire enabled the pilot of the chopper to guide the missile mid-air before impact. This wiring could sometimes extend for several kilometers. The helicopters had shot so many missiles that the entire Gaza Strip was covered with a grid of strong, thin, copper wire. Every night someone tripped and fell flat on their face from one of these wires.

As we were advancing Danny-Boy suddenly disappeared from view.

"Axl! Axl!" My Canadian friend heard a voice hiss at him seemingly from nowhere. "Don't just stand there! Help me!"

It was then that Axl saw the head and arm of Danny-Boy protruding from a hole in the ground. He had fallen into the entrance of a Hamas tunnel. Axl ran over to him and helped him out. He then reported the tunnel to the officers.

One of the greatest threats to Israel from the Gaza Strip was their complex network of tunnels. These tunnels were used for weapons smuggling and storage. Even more frightening, however, was their usage to kidnap and/or kill soldiers. I heard the following account from a tank officer I knew.

The tank officer, "Bob," was sitting in the cockpit of his *Merkava* tank with one of his crewmen, "Joe." They scanned the area for threats with thermal vision.

"Hey, Joe, do you see that on the thermal screen? There's something coming out of the ground over there."

"Yeah, Bob, I think it's a gopher or something."

"No... I don't think so. But... what is it?"

"Wait a minute, Joe, do you see that!"

Bob and Joe watched the thermal viewing screen. Just fifty meters in front of them a shovel popped out of a small hole in the ground. A human hand soon followed, groping the entrance of the tunnel and attempting to widen it.

Bob quickly and quietly waltzed over to the small hole. He tossed a hand grenade inside and ran.

And that was the end of a squad of Hamas terrorists. The tank officer and his crew inspected the site. They found a newly dug tunnel connected to the preexisting underground passage system. It was apparent that this Hamas team had the intention of kidnapping the tank crew just like Gilad Shalit. Unfortunately for them they made a mistake with the digging and surfaced just in front of the tank and their intended targets.

Immediately prior to Operation: Cast Lead Axl had been given the impromptu specialty of firing the Matador weapon after a very brief training course. There wasn't much I could say about the Matador beyond that it was a brand-new shoulder-mounted rocket. But I could say that, to my knowledge, Axl made history by being the first soldier of any army to fire the Matador rocket in a combat situation.

It was near dawn and we had entered even further into the Gaza Strip. I was already exhausted from a night of combat and no sleep. But there was more to come...

Day 15. January 17th, 2009: Withdrawal

We were exhausted. The whole night had been consumed by our assault from the beach. Now it was daylight. We were stationed in one of the Hamas houses we had attacked and conquered. Although the house was relatively large it simply was not large enough for all the soldiers inside to sleep comfortably. My attempts to doze off a little between watches were unsuccessful. I went into a little girl's bedroom trying to find a comfortable place to nap. The whole house had been all but destroyed. Shards of glass and pieces of plaster littered the floor. I examined the lines of bullet holes scattered throughout the walls. Then I noticed an enormous orange stuffed rabbit, almost like a giant Care-Bear with long ears, sitting on a large shelf.

"Hey, Shaft! Look, you monster! You killed it!"

Sure enough, the giant rabbit was riddled with bullet holes from his MAG 7.62mm machine gun. The stuffing had been tossed about the room. The rabbit hunched over, its eyes cold and lifeless. War was an ugly thing.

There was another doll on the shelf. This doll was unharmed, but its head was positioned against the wall exactly between two bullet holes.

While marveling at the good fortune bestowed upon this toy Captain America called me and Axl to the top floor. We had enemy contacts. Four Hamas terrorists attempted an assault from a nearby house. We set up defensive positions and prepared for a counterstrike.

I set up my M4 with Trijicon scope in a window, functioning as a relatively short-range sniper. I scanned the doors and windows with my finger on the trigger. Meanwhile, the tanks surrounded the three or four-story building they occupied. Likewise, a demolitions crew moved in. They no longer needed me to snipe them. We were going to blow up the entire house.

I sat back and watched, covering the approach of the demolitions team. Numerous tanks sat in the streets and alleys, with the cannons aimed at the house. The demolitions crew placed charges on the corners of the house.

The demolitions crew set off the explosives in conjunction with an enormous salvo from at least half a dozen tanks. In a matter of seconds there was very little left of the house or terrorists.

To my surprise we continued pushing forward, but now in broad daylight. We usually preferred to operate at night. Our platoon moved from house to house, mansion to mansion, checking for terrorists and weapons.

We entered yet another beautiful Hamas home. We made our entry shooting and lobbing grenades. As I entered I surveyed the damage to the marble pillars and expensive statuettes. In the living room was an aquarium full of exotic fish. To my surprise the fish tank was unscratched despite the excessive damage all around it. One of the soldiers even fed the fish before we left.

Searching the house I entered another little girl's room. Judging by the photos of her as well as the size of her clothes she couldn't have been more than seven years old. In her room we found the ultra-violent computer game, Grand Theft Auto, a collection of Steven Segal movies, as well as a collection of sharp barber-style razors. Apparently Hamas parenting techniques did not frown upon inundating their small children with violent entertainment and likewise allowed them to play with razors.

I moved to the roof of a neighboring house to cover the approach of Platoon Eight. I surveyed the view. In the distance I saw a large mosque toppled over and destroyed. I remembered hearing about it a few days previously. Hamas had used the mosque to store huge quantities of weapons and had booby trapped the structure to the point of making any entry suicidal. We placed charges on the mosque to take out the weapons. But there were so many munitions inside that the entire mosque collapsed on itself. It was now reduced to a pile of rubble with the gigantic dome rolled off to the side.

We continued to advance. I went up ahead, shooting out locks and kicking in doors. Evening drew near and we entered a new mansion and prepared for nightfall.

It was about ten in the evening and suddenly we began hearing rumors from the medics and doctors. They began making preparations to evacuate the house. There were rumors of a cease-fire. I didn't believe it. Even if there would be a cease-fire it would take time to implement it and finalize the deal and the removal of Israeli forces would not be a simple process.

I was wrong. At midnight we received orders to prepare for a full and immediate withdrawal. We were to move out in two hours, at two in the morning. And we would be walking the entire distance from the edge of Gaza City to the Israeli border, and then to the nearby IDF military base where it had all begun.

The attitudes and responses to the cease-fire were varied. Some of us just wanted to go home and didn't care what that meant for the overall picture. Some of us were disappointed, disagreeing with the cease-fire and finding it a weak decision. Some of us were simply warriors, and didn't know what to do when there wasn't a war of some kind. I sat in a corner of the Hamas mansion. I asked Smirnoff for a cigarette. I didn't smoke and it had been one of my only cigarettes in over a year. It seemed like an appropriate time but it didn't really help. I was very upset. I was not a politician and it was not my purpose to involve myself in the political situation. But it seemed like failure. We were winning. Hamas was unable to stand before us, before *me*. I watched terrorists flee from me in horror. Those that didn't soon became rotting carcasses in my path. I felt unstoppable. We were in a position to destroy fifteen years of terrorist development and weapon smuggling. In my opinion we would have been able to get Gilad Shalit back without the ridiculous negotiations of trading one thousand terrorists for one of our soldiers.

We were in the position to *smash* Hamas, to wipe a murderous terrorist organization off the face of the earth. And now we were being told to stop, to pack it all up and go home.

It is a severe violation of my over-inflated ego to admit it but I will. I actually cried.

I thought about Cocoa Puff, my friend shaking in the bomb shelter. I thought about Sergeant Obama and his family trying to live in Ashkelon, even after a missile had landed on their block. I thought about Lieutenant Aharon Karov with shrapnel in his brain, lying half-conscious in a hospital with his newly-wed wife sitting in a chair next to him. I thought about my apartment and wondered if it even still existed or if it had been destroyed by Grad missiles. I thought about all the people I had killed. I thought about all the people who had been trying to kill me.

Had it all been for nothing?

It felt like failure. It felt like betrayal.

No one else in the platoon reacted as strongly as I did. Those of us with a little broader perspective were also unhappy, including Axl, Shaft, and the officers. Captain America and Sergeant Obama both pulled me aside later. They both gave me a speech of patronization. Yeah, yeah. We had hit Hamas hard and all that. The final score card was tallied up with over nine hundred Hamas terrorists dead and roughly two hundred and fifty civilian casualties.[1] About thirteen Israeli soldiers had been killed and at least four of them had died from friendly-fire. That meant we had a kill ratio of approximately one hundred to one with less than twenty-two percent civilian casualties. But I wasn't stupid. I knew that we had hit them hard but it would only be a matter of time before they would start firing missiles and rockets again. I expected a month or two of calm and then renewed violence.[2]

I tossed the half-finished cigarette away and we began marching the eight kilometers back to the border.

We followed a route on the beach where the water met the sand. Several times a freak wave danced on the shore and filled my red boots with salt water. The entire army marched silently in double-file. It was surreal, listening to the waves crash in the darkness. I hoped that the D9 bulldozers had successfully cleared all the mines in our path.

Walking along I spotted an odd shape in the water just past the breaking waves. I peered at it through my night vision scope.

It was hard to be sure in the darkness, but it appeared to be a dead body, washed up on the beach with the endless waves breaking over it. Having grown up near the ocean in Los Angeles I was quite familiar with the breaking waves serving as a physical metaphor of eternity. For better or for worse, this individual had already made his journey into the world beyond.

We moved on. Just before the border we took a brief break. I leaned back against my equipment and sat on the sand. For the entire war I had been saving a single can of Coca-Cola until the end as a celebratory treat. I had actually Jerry-rigged one of my magazine pouches to hold the cola can and protect it from puncture. This was hardly the way I had wanted the war to end but I

[1] These figures were still being debated, but this was the official IDF report. IDF Estimate: 900 combatants, 250 civilians (and all women and minors were considered civilians regardless of their actual role in the conflict, even if they were armed threats). Hamas estimated that 700 combatants and 750 civilians were killed. It should be noted that critics of Israel consistently accuse us of "disproportionate response", "reckless killing of civilians", and even "genocidal motives." However, even using the Hamas figures the IDF was running at a rate of roughly fifty percent civilian casualties, which was not considered "reckless" or a "war crime" according to international law. Using Israeli estimates we were operating at a rate of about twenty-two percent civilian casualties. Also, as far "genocidal motives" were concerned, about one-tenth of one percent (0.1%) of the population of the Gaza Strip was killed in Operation: Cast Lead. Such being

the case this was by far the most unsuccessful genocide attempt in human history (and therefore obviously *not* an attempt at genocide.) And again, these estimates are based on Hamas figures that even pro-Palestinian Arab proponents in the United Nations dismissed as being exaggerated as propaganda.

When the Russian military invaded Chechnya repeatedly they killed a total of 20,000 – 40,000 combatants and maintained a non-combatant death toll of over 200,000 civilians. There have also been estimates of over 20,000 of these civilian casualties being children. (These figures are still being argued. However, these are considered the "conservative" estimates purported by the Russian-Chechen Friendship Society.) This meant that they were operating at a rate of 80-90% civilian casualties. Additionally, there were less people living in Chechnya than the Gaza Strip, and at least one-fifth (over 20%) of the civilian population was slaughtered by the Russian advance. Compare these estimates to the 900 combatants, 250 civilians (IDF) or 700 combatants, 750 civilians (Hamas) of Operation: Cast Lead. And compare 20% of the population of Chechnya being killed as opposed to 0.1% of the Gaza Strip (excluding Yehudah V'Shomron, or the West Bank). Also, from the time of Operation: Cast Lead and the decade leading up to it the total Palestinian Arab casualty toll, both combatant and civilian, was about 5,500 people. In short, for every single Palestinian Arab that died in the Gaza Strip and/or Yehudah V' Shomron (the West Bank) at the hands of the IDF over the course of a decade at least forty Chechens were killed by the Russian military during two military operations, or 1:40.

It should also be noted that in this model the Russian-Chechen conflict was used, in which Russia was viewed as a supposedly "semi-responsible" world power. If the estimates of 300,000 dead and 2,000,000 displaced Sudanese black Africans by the genocidal Moslem Arab government of Sudan were analyzed the statistics were *far* worse. The figures came out to one Palestinian Arab death to at least fifty five Sudanese Africans dying, or 1:55. In other words *if* the IDF were to go into the Gaza Strip, randomly kill one out of every four persons we encountered, and drive the rest of the Palestinian Arabs into the Sinai we *still* would *not* have done what has *already been done* by Moslem Arabs in the Sudan.

So the obvious question was this: Why did the world care so much about the fate of Palestinian Arabs to the point of demonizing Israel and yet ignored legitimate atrocities committed in other regions by other governments? That would be my point exactly.]

[² It turned out that they waited even less time than that, seriously violating the cease-fire repeatedly within a mere few weeks.]

figured it was over anyway. I sat next to Sergeant Obama. He heard the unmistakable "hiss and pop" of a can of Coca-Cola being opened.

"No way..." he whispered. I took the first sip, smiled with satisfaction, and passed it to him. The single can of Coca-Cola made its way down the line through the platoon. It was worth its weight in gold.

Nothin' like the real thing.

We crossed the border and re-entered friendly territory. The press was there with numerous *jobnik* (non-combat) girls taking photos. Most of the guys in the platoon tried to make it look good for the camera. I ignored them and kept walking. I still felt like we had failed, given up, and saw no point in celebration.

Finally we arrived at a large parking lot just outside of the base where it had all began. For the first time in over two weeks I was able to take off my combat vest and body armor. I felt so light. I also realized that I was in desperate need of a chiropractor. I took off my helmet. I was still wearing the purple bandana.

"Hey, Killswitch," a friend of mine called from a different company in the Paratroopers. "What's up with the bandana?"

I examined the bandana. The personal messages were still there, semi-blurred from mud and sweat. I thought about all of my friends back home.

"It's a long story..." I responded quietly. I was tired of explaining it.

I looked around the parking lot. All of my friends were there. We were all coming back. It was so good to see the faces of them all. Some were better, some were worse. All were tired and dirty. I saw one of my former sergeants. Somewhere along the line his pants had been torn apart. Not much was left and we all laughed at his exposed boxer shorts.

I saw a group of religious soldiers pray. It was their first *Shachrit* (morning prayer) back on our side of the fence and without the danger of being bombed.

I saw Cueball. He somehow had gotten hold of a cell phone and called his parents back in the United States. They hadn't heard anything about him or from him the entire war. I found out later that they first found out that he was in the Gaza Strip because of my blog on the internet.

We listened to a speech from the head colonel, commander of the entire Paratrooper Brigade. I was sure that it must have been timely and inspiring but I honestly had no memory of what he said. I was too tired to pay attention. I hadn't slept in days, fighting and marching non-stop for the past two nights.

I returned to the area where we had left our equipment. I lay down on the hard asphalt in the warm early morning sun, using my combat vest as a pillow. I had never felt anything so wonderfully relaxing. I immediately passed out, waiting for the military buses to take us back to our main base.

Days 16 & 17. January 18th-19th, 2009: The Final Post

It was morning. After my brief nap on the asphalt we returned to the base where we had waited for a week to go in. We were still on maximum alert so our first priority was to check and prepare all our equipment. We cleaned our guns, refilled our magazines, and replaced all other supplies depleted during the war.

Then we went to the showers; nice, hot, fresh, steaming showers. It was even more wonderful than the asphalt. But there was a problem. The Gaza Strip was very dirty. And not all of the houses we stayed in were Hamas mansions. I was covered with fleas and possibly lice. To me there was only one reasonable solution. I shaved every hair off of my entire body, from my head to my toes. I looked like a naked mole rat.

Finally all equipment was more or less prepared and I was clean. They gave us our cell phones back and I checked my voice mail.

Cocoa Puff, the girl who had been shaking in the bomb shelter, had left me eleven voice messages, almost crying in each one. I was relatively surprised. We weren't dating, or at least, not in an official sense. I did not expect that kind of response from anyone except maybe a girlfriend. I guess that was one indicator of many that our officially "unofficial" status was evolving into something more after all.

After listening to all the messages I began calling my friends. I was exhausted but I tried carrying on a conversation. They asked me how it was.

"Well," I answered. "It was... a war."

I didn't really have anything to say. I honestly hadn't really thought about it. I had been in an automatic mode governed by instinct for so long that I hadn't actually *thought* about anything. It wasn't until then that I really began thinking about it. I began to remember.

Did I really just survive all that? Did I really just do all that?

Eventually I got off the phone and found a bed. It was such a sweet sleep.

The next morning I was awakened by my lieutenant, Captain America. The previous day I had tried to make a deal with him to go home early. He told me he would have an answer for me in the morning. He woke me up with his answer.

"Yes, Killswitch. Go home."

I made a few touch-ups to my equipment. Then I switched to my dress uniform, grabbed my bag, and made my way home. I climbed onto the bus. Sitting on the bus it occurred to me that my *kippah* (*yarmulke*, or Jewish head covering) was missing. It had been borrowed for morning prayer and I had never gotten it back. I reached into my pocket, hoping to find my spare. It wasn't there, but I smiled at what I found. It was my purple bandana.

Well, I needed something on my head. So I put the bandana back on my now shiny, fully-shaved head. For a brief moment it felt like the whole world was laughing at me. There I was, back in the real world, with shaved legs and a purple bandana tied pirate-style on my head. But then I realized that I just didn't really care. I had just fought a war and won. As far as I was concerned the world could laugh at me all they wanted.

On the bus I thought about the internet blog. Using my internet phone I looked up the site, curious to see if anything was going on with it. I was in shock.

For one entry alone there were over sixty-two comments. I couldn't believe it. I hadn't even done anything yet. Had that many people actually been reading my rambling and actually commented on it? I hoped that as many other soldiers as possible had also read the comments. I hoped that they also saw how many people prayed for us and supported us.

It was evening and I arrived at my kibbutz, still wearing the bandana. I saw my married friend who had given it to me. But now she was wearing a dark green bandana.

"What?" I exclaimed. "Wait a minute! You mean to tell me that I have been running all over the Gaza Strip with this wimpy, purple bandana on my head, and this whole time you have been sitting here with a dark green one?!"

She laughed and offered to trade.

"No," I replied thoughtfully. "The wimpy, purple one is actually starting to grow on me."

Then I saw Cocoa Puff. She came over to my apartment and immediately went into my cupboard, digging through my perpetual supply of alcohol and chocolate. We opened a bottle of red wine and she helped herself to my precious supply of Reese's Peanut Cups that I had imported from the United States.[1] We sat on my bed and talked about the war for a while.

And then... she left.

I'm not sure what I was expecting but it wasn't that. I sat on my bed alone and stared at the half-drunk bottle of wine and the chocolate wrappers littering the floor.

The spoils of war were overrated.

Later I hopped on a bus to Jerusalem to meet up with my friends for coffee in the city center. It was so good and yet so strange to see them all again. Some of them had even gotten married in the time that I was gone. I had wanted to attend the wedding but obviously had been unable.

I sat in the warm coffee shop and drank a gigantic, delicious iced mocha. Then my friends suddenly broke out into song and presented me with a small chocolate cake complete with a single candle on top.

"Happy birthday to you, happy birthday..."

The war had started on my Gregorian birthday, and my Hebrew birthday had been a few days after. I had forgotten all about it. My friends hadn't.

I smiled with contentment at my friends, my little cake, and my iced mocha. For one night, if only one night, I could forget about guns, hand grenades, war, killing, and terrorists. For at least one night I could enjoy myself as a twenty-four year old.

Yes, it was good to be alive.

But unfortunately the story didn't end here. Hamas had already violated the cease-fire many times. My apartment was located near a large air force base. From my bedroom window I could see the F-15's rise into the sky. The bottoms of the jets were heavily loaded with bombs and missiles. I was watching them kick on the afterburners and scream towards the Gaza Strip. In a few hours I would check the news and read about the air strikes as well as the rockets, missiles, and mortars landing on Israeli cities from Hamas. I was almost waiting for Captain America to call me on my cell phone and cancel my vacation.

[1 Reese's Peanut Butter Cups were very difficult to find here in Israel.]

I knew that this wouldn't be the end. I firmly believed that as long as I served in the IDF, both as an active duty soldier as well as a reservist later, I would one day return to the Gaza Strip.

February 15th, 2009: Success of the Blog

The blog was extremely successful and popular. The head editor of Chabad.org told me that they had never had a publication this successful before. It was averaging over 27,000 hits per day. The link was also immediately placed on the front/home page of the website.

I was absolutely thrilled that Chabad.org worked with me to get the blog up. They gave me an incredible opportunity to get my writing out, tell my story, express my views, and help support the soldiers of the IDF. And the publishing staff was always *extremely* helpful and courteous, going to great lengths to work with me in every way possible. So I want to say a *huge* "Thank You!" to all the staff at Chabad.org and in particular to Chana W. and Dovid Z.

Soon I started talking to my friends who had likewise been involved and began swapping stories. Foxtrot, a Canadian soldier in Givati that I had studied with on my kibbutz, had been there in a different area. While preparing to clear a house he had been shot by a sniper. He was a *Negevist* (similar to an American SAW, or Squad Automatic Weapon, medium machine gunner). The sniper bullet struck a rolled-up belt of bullets in the front of his combat vest and then smashed into his ceramic armor. The bullet did not penetrate the body armor. But he was knocked to the ground, received a mild concussion, and somehow scratched both of his eyes in the process.

I never ascertained exactly how he managed to scratch *both* eyes. Regardless, he was immediately evacuated from the Gaza Strip. In the military hospital he received multiple donations and was even flown around the world to "tell his story." He was pampered with delicious kosher banquets and five-star hotels. When I finally returned from the Gaza Strip my cell phone inbox was full of photos of *his* "spoils of war."

Foxtrot used the incident of his being "wounded in action" to try to obtain both sympathy and phone numbers from beautiful young Jewish women. He usually succeeded in neither. On one occasion in particular we were drinking beers in a bar and he went into his whole dramatic (and exaggerated) story, attempting to impress an attractive young woman.

"That's amazing," she breathed to Foxtrot. " And you're so brave! I'm so glad you're okay. And Killswitch, did you get shot or hurt?"

"No," I replied while rolling my eyes and trying to avoid vomiting. "I was always smart enough to *duck* every time they were shooting at me."

On a similar occasion he again began to brag about his "being shot" and "wounds of war." I finally countered with the truth, pointing out that he had merely scratched his eyes.

"Yeah," he stammered, "but those scratches hurt! I was an out-patient of that hospital and had to use prescription eye drops for *two weeks* because that happened."

My lieutenant, Captain America, called me and canceled my weekend leave. In all fairness he made a reasonable deal with me and I would get a few extra days off next week, so it worked out for me in the end. But it meant that I had to pack up my stuff and immediately return to my new post on the Lebanese border.

PART IX: THIRD DEPLOYMENT
LEBANESE BORDER

March 18th, 2009: Post-Traumatic Stress Disorder

Not long after Operation: Cast Lead I was due for a ten day leave from the IDF. It was a strange feeling to be on vacation after the war. I was still in war mode in a lot of ways. Even just walking down the street and going to a local sidewalk café I found myself sitting in a corner and checking the nearby windows for snipers and other threats.

My friends said that I acted differently as well. They claimed it was something in my eyes, something about the way I walked. I guess once I had been exposed to that kind of violence, killed people, and watched my friends get shot, there was no going back.

I had been having a lot of weird dreams as well. They weren't nightmares necessarily, but they were definitely very violent in nature.

Another weird effect of the war was that my appeal to the opposite gender had multiplied dramatically. I never had problems getting girls, as was obvious. But now I couldn't get rid of them. Evidently, after staring death in the face and surviving my self-confidence increased significantly.

One example of this facet was Cocoa Puff. Before the war we had been "normal" friends and had started to venture into the realm of "more than friends." After the war, however, it was more than obvious that there was very little remaining of our "normal" friendship. Almost all the time I was away from the military I spent with her. I took her out to dinner, to movies, to my friends' weddings, etc. A certain amount of physical affection ensued as well. The only catch was that she was studying in a religious course on our kibbutz and they didn't really like the girls having boyfriends. So we kept everything quiet and unofficial. But I was okay with that. It was less gossip anyway. But even so everyone considered us to be together.

So in the month of February I was at the top of my game. I had fought a war and won. I was considered a "hero." I had finally done something worthwhile in my military career. I was a published author with my war diary getting 27,000 hits a day. I had been approached about publishing my book. And I had a beautiful Latin girl waiting for me every time I got a weekend off from the army.

As aforementioned I had made a deal with my lieutenant to get my vacation a little early. The deal was that I was supposed to return to our base and guard it while everyone else was on vacation at the normal time. It was actually a great plan. I got my nine days at home, came back to our base in the Golan Heights, and pretended to guard while the rest of the battalion went on their nine day vacation. The few of us that remained sat around and did *nothing* for nine days. We even got permission from our commander to sneak off the base and go to a pub on a nearby kibbutz. Obviously if a high-ranking officer had caught us we would have gone to jail. But all of the officers were at home with their families. Being stupid, however, wasn't really my thing. It wasn't that I was a goody-goody so much as I didn't think one beer was worth jail time. I personally passed the time by making mini-movies with the fellow guys on our camera phones. And I soon discovered that a military base hosted a wide variety of amazing props for such an endeavor.

About this time we had elections for the prime minister here in Israel. They brought a ballot system to the base where we were at and set it up in the office of the major. As I waited in line to vote the thought suddenly occurred to me that I could have a lot of fun with the voting personnel.

Here in Israel we utilized an unusual voting system. Basically we were presented with a variety of small, white, square pieces of paper with the names of the candidates and their corresponding political parties. In Israel there were numerous political parties to choose from, not just two primary parties like in the United States. We then selected the appropriate piece of paper and placed it in an envelope, sealed it, and dropped it into the ballot box. We then signed a separate form that we did indeed vote.

When I entered the office I said in Hebrew with the worst American accent I could muster (which wasn't hard, considering how bad my accent was anyway),

"Excuse me, but I don't really know what to do here. Could you explain it to me?"

They then explained the system and handed me an envelope. I took it and examined it.

"But it's empty," I complained.

"Yeah, you're supposed to put something in it."

"Oh, okay." Then I walked over to the rack of voting squares and examined the corresponding chart of which initials indicated which candidate and which party. I called a nineteen year-old *jobnik* (non-combat) girl over and asked,

"How do I vote for Golda Meir?"[1]

I heard the voting personnel start snickering behind me but I kept a straight face. To my shock the girl actually started looking for Golda Meir on the chart. And I thought I was ignorant of Israeli politics. I was the American immigrant!

When she couldn't find it I then asked about Moshe Katsav.[2] The *jobnik* girl *did* know who he was and rather awkwardly replied that he wasn't running.

I walked over to the pieces of paper and then asked, "Okay, so how many can I choose?"

"Um... just one."

"Only one? Well then how am I supposed to decide?"

Of course, I knew exactly what I was doing and exactly who I wanted to vote for. But in a show I shrugged and said, "Oh, whatever" and grabbed a note. The ballot collectors thought I just randomly picked a candidate to vote for. I got a good laugh out of it all.

When the battalion came back from their vacation we started our winter war training. As if it wasn't enough that we had just actually fought a winter war we were going to train for another one. At first I started to complain about it. But then after thinking about it I remembered that we were combat soldiers and this was what combat soldiers did: train.

Winter war training was difficult simply because of the weather conditions. Summer war training had the problem of heat. But at night the temperature cooled down and was actually rather pleasant. The IDF traditionally conducted its operations and accordingly training in the night hours. But in the winter we froze. And believe it or not, in the Golan Heights it actually could snow. Worse than snow, I discovered, was cold rain.

[1] Golda Meir was the female prime minister of Israel back in the early 1970's during the time of the 1972 Munich massacre of the Israeli olympians and the Yom Kippur War of 1973. Voting for her in 2009 would have been the equivalent of trying to vote for Abraham Lincoln during the 2008 Obama vs. McCain election.]

[2] Moshe Katsav was the recent president (similar to the American vice-president) who had been removed from office on unconfirmed accusation of corruption and rape.]

One thing I didn't really understand about war training was why we did so much marching. Ninety percent or more of the training involved moving from point A to B with large amounts of equipment on our backs. I understood that it was important. But after having been in the military for two years I just felt like saying, "Yeah, yeah, walking with a lot of heavy stuff on my back for ten kilometers. I get it already!"

But then life threw me a little bit of a curve ball. Somewhere along the line, most likely in the Gaza Strip, I had contracted Swine Flu or some derivative thereof.[1] And the winter war training lowered my immune system enough to bring it out in full fury. I came back from the training and immediately started vomiting eight times in a row right in front of my commanders and officers. There were a lot of ways to fake being sick but it was pretty difficult to fake incessant vomiting. I also had horrific diarrhea, very high fever, a nasty cough, and heavy congestion. I couldn't keep any water down, let alone any food in my stomach. I survived by Smirnoff the medic giving me incessant IV's.

The military doctors, however, were simply idiotic. Because so many soldiers did fake being sick they kept assuming that I was faking, too. The situation was highly annoying. One doctor claimed that it was food poisoning. Another doctor said it was spring time allergies. Both doctors openly said they thought I was probably faking anyway and gave me a slip that confined me to "office work" for the next three days. Now as the lead designated marksman of a missile platoon in the IDF Paratroopers in the middle of Winter War Training what kind of "office work" did the doctors honestly think I would be doing?

It took me over a month to fully recover from it all. By the end of it all I lost about fourteen kilograms (over thirty pounds)! And it showed, too. Towards the end Captain America finally got the doctors to realize there was something genuinely wrong with me after he yelled at them for weeks. They sent me to a military hospital to do a long list of checks, everything from blood tests to stool

[1] It was later speculated that I had contracted an early strain of Swine Flu, thereby explaining the severity of the illness and inability to identify it. It was about this time that Mexico City became heavily infected. It was theorized that Swine Flu did not begin in Mexico City, but rather first reached epidemic level there and was accordingly identified. However, there were reports of persons suffering from a similar illness all over the world, particularly Europe. So the conclusion was that Swine Flu originated elsewhere and spread, and that due to poor hygienic conditions and a lack of quality healthcare Mexico City was hit far harder than Europe and attracted the most attention.]

samples. They never did figure out on an official level what was wrong with me. Or, if they did, they never bothered to tell me.

Right before the Jewish holiday of Purim we were scheduled for a three day weekend leave starting with Thursday morning and ending Sunday morning. We were all excited to finally get to go home. We were planning on being on a bus out of the base by eight in the morning. But at five in the morning Major Bloodlust woke us all up and made us stand in formation for a briefing. Apparently one of our Druze Arab soldiers had lost his custom night vision monocular. If night vision goggles were lost or stolen then the soldier responsible for them was given a serious trial and jail sentence, much more than if he had punched the major himself in the face. Major Bloodlust informed us that no one was going home until they found the night vision monocular. So we all had to look for it. This Druze Arab soldier wasn't even part of my platoon; therefore we weren't connected at all. But the entire company had been locked down. To make it worse the Druze soldier himself wasn't even on the base. He was already home due to a family emergency.

The entire company tore the base apart and couldn't find it. We saw the military buses come and go at eight in the morning and take all the other soldiers in the battalion home. Meanwhile, we were still stuck on the base. The Druze soldier came back to base and immediately went to sleep in one of the barracks without even bothering to look for it himself.

At three in the afternoon the officers finally decided to let us go home. The Druze soldier was simply going to be put on trial and suffer the consequences. At this point he had already sneaked off base and gone back home. I was standing and waiting for the military bus to pull up. Being sick, feverish, and weak I went over to a nearby Hummer to sit down for a few minutes. Brushing mud off of the seat of the driver's side what did I spy next to the gas pedal? The missing night vision monocular.[1]

I let out a loud string of profanity consisting of four languages. *After* we had received permission to go home anyway *then* I found it. And the Druze soldier and his platoon didn't think about checking the Hummers. Sunday morning came and I was far too ill to go back to the army. My lieutenant told me to stay home even without doctor permission, which wasunheard of in the IDF.

[1 Even though I had saved him from a jail sentence and nasty fine I never got any thanks or words of gratitude. Sometimes I just couldn't handle the stupidity of some of the people around me.]

Captain America was awesome, what could I say? It was now Purim. Purim was a Jewish holiday that commemorated the story of Esther and Mordechai and how they saved the Jewish people from genocide at the hand of Haman. It consisted of reading the scroll of Esther, wearing costumes, and consuming large quantities of alcohol.

I was so sick I couldn't celebrate. My adoptive family wanted to take me to the hospital even. The only reason I didn't was because my military insurance wouldn't pay for it. I would have had to gone to a military hospital, but that was much more difficult than it sounded. The kibbutz doctor looked at me and gave me some medication but likewise couldn't do too much because of the insurance problem.

Purim was here and the entire kibbutz and the whole country was partying. Meanwhile, I was rotting alone in my apartment. And it was this night that I discovered that my nice, beautiful, sweet little Latin Cocoa Puff had turned on me. After I had spent the last half year taking care of her to the best of my ability she left me alone all night in my apartment. It was Purim, I understood that. But I soon discovered that she had been trying to seduce at least one of my friends. She used our officially "unofficial" status as an excuse. She even claimed that she wasn't a "mind-reader" and "had no idea" that sleeping with my fellow soldiers and kibbutz volunteers would upset me. Needless to say, that was the end of our undefined relationship.

I had just gone to the Gaza Strip and stepped over the bodies of dead terrorists only to be publicly humiliated by a twenty year-old Central American girl. I couldn't even believe it.

About the same time the aftershock of the war and post-traumatic stress disorder (PTSD) hit me. I went into a state of extreme depression. Adding to it all was the fact that Cocoa Puff still wouldn't go away. I never understood why the girl who had used excuse after excuse to avoid an official relationship and had been sleeping with other people couldn't accept the idea that I was unhappy with her and had moved on. Several family issues blew up in my face as well.

In the month of February I was a hero with a beautiful girl waiting for me to come home each weekend leave. In the month of March I was considered little more than a drunkard and a loser in dating. I was alone, sicker than I had ever been in my life, and had flashbacks from the war pounding in my head incessantly.

It was interesting to note the position of a warrior in society. We were misunderstood, feared, loathed, despised, and rejected until society needed us to protect them from a threat. We risked our lives, even died, to save their lives. And then after it all we eventually returned to our status of being rejected, avoided, and cast off by the society we protected. Until, of course, another threat posed itself. Then the cycle repeated itself.

People simply did not understand the mental and emotional state that a professional soldier had to keep himself in to be the best at what he did. A warrior could flip a switch and kill an enemy efficiently and without emotion for a reason. But in reaching that psychological state the personality of the warrior obviously suffered side effects.

I was really surprised at how hard I took the incident with Cocoa Puff. It probably had more to do with the post-traumatic stress disorder than anything. It wasn't like me to get *that* attached to a girl. My friends commented later that they noticed themselves being more emotional than usual as well. Somehow I always thought PTSD would have had the opposite effect. Apparently not.

May 1st, 2009: The Multiple Love Letter Incident

After completing a brief course in Tel Aviv I received permission at the last minute to go to Rio's military ceremony. Rio was my friend of three years from Brazil and my Australian roommate's girlfriend. She was now a *jobnik* (non-combat) girl who worked with computers and was finishing her training course. I wanted to surprise her so I took down the basic details of her ceremony from her cousin.

I arrived at her base and even bought her a bouquet of yellow friendship roses.[1] I found her in the dining hall. She gave me a big hug when she saw me, asking in surprise, "What are you doing here?"

"I'm here for your ceremony obviously," I responded.

"But that's not today. That's *next* Tuesday."

I had just wandered an IDF base with roses for half an hour for nothing.

"Hey, wait a second," I said after a long succession of profanity. "It was your birthday a few days ago, wasn't it? So, um... Happy Birthday!"

But now I was waiting for the inevitable conversation between my roommate, Toohey, and his girlfriend, Rio...

"Hey, baby. What's with the roses?"

"Your roommate gave them to me."

Fortunately for me he thought it was even funnier than I did.

About this time a new volunteer group came to the kibbutz. As stated earlier my game with females had been at an all-time high lately, even when I went into my month-long depression. At least five of the girls were obsessed with me. Maybe the uniform got to them. At first I liked the attention. But it didn't take very long for me to realize that these girls were all incredibly annoying, especially

[1 I honestly wasn't so interested in giving her the flowers. The idea was more that I wanted her cute friends to see the "nice guy giving his casual friend flowers" and make a good impression.]

because I was still in my negative-emotion mode. They started calling me all the time (I wasn't sure how they even got my phone number) and inviting themselves over to my apartment. This new trend was the last thing that I wanted when I was depressed. All I wanted to do was sit in my apartment, drink beer, listen to my hard rock and heavy metal music, and occasionally smoke a cigarette.

It was April Fool's Day and I came up with a brilliant plan. I wrote a long sappy love letter consisting of completely ridiculous clichés such as, "I can't stop thinking about you," "from the first time I saw you I was consumed by your beauty," and "I can't even sleep at night because I'm thinking about you." I then ended the letter with "But *please* don't tell anyone that I sent you this letter!"

I then copied and pasted it and sent the exact same letter to five different girls via Facebook. To make it worse I even started a poll with my military friends as to how long it would take for these five girls to figure out what I had done with the grand prize being a six pack of beer. I put my money on twenty-four hours.

Three and a half hours later there was a small riot in the *ulpan* (Hebrew study program) dormitories, with half a dozen girls enraged at the discovery that I had made "April Fools" out of them. Unfortunately, however, this meant that I didn't win the six pack of beer after all.

June 12th, 2009: Minefields in Lebanon

After the Multiple Love Letter incident I fled the kibbutz and returned to our current front line: The Lebanese Border.

The Lebanese Border was a unique front line because it was both dangerous and boring at the same time. Along the entire border was an electronic fence similar to the fence surrounding the Gaza Strip. The problem was that the weather conditions and local wildlife caused significantly more problems with the fence than outside of the Gaza Strip. At least five times a day the alarms went off, alerting us that something or someone was trying to climb the fence. We would hear the code *"Chava Adoma"* ("Red Farm") called out over the intercom or the radio incessantly. Correspondingly, we would race out to the scene in our armored Hummers usually to find absolutely nothing. Occasionally we saw a few wild boars or other animals. Every time these animals tried to get past the fence and enter into Lebanon or vice-versa it set off the alarms. Likewise, different weather conditions often caused the fence to malfunction.

But Lebanon itself was absolutely beautiful. It reminded me of something one would find in Tolkein's *Lord of the Rings.* Small mountains were covered with rolling green grass and cedar forests. In the morning there was always a layer of fog and mist, with the small peaks peeping through into the sunshine. But all of that was inevitably ruined by Hezbollah and the Palestinian Arabs. The Palestinian Arabs had caused too many problems for the Jordanian kingdom back in the late 1960's. Accordingly, many of the militants were driven out in September of 1970. They formed a variety of terror cells, one of which was called Black September after the Jordanian expulsion. These Palestinian Arab terrorist organizations had harassed and often slaughtered Lebanese Christian political groups and assassinated their leaders for decades, forcing many of them to flee. With most of the Lebanese Christians displaced from the southern regions the Palestinian Arabs, as well as Hezbollah, focused their attention on attacking Israeli military and civilian targets. Hezbollah, a Lebanese Moslem terrorist organization supported by Iran and Syria, also attacked American military targets, killing well over two hundred American Marines in Beirut in the early 1980's. In short, the Palestinian Arab terror cells and their allies had effectively destroyed one of the most beautiful areas of the Middle East and it was nothing short of tragic.

Between Israel and Lebanon the United Nations had placed "peacekeeping" forces. In our area there were mainly troops from Nepal, Spain, and Poland. The Nepalese always cracked me up. When we passed by in patrols along the border they always peeped out at us from their bunkers and guard towers. I always waved from the mounted MAG 7.62mm machine gun on our armored Hummer. They usually saluted me back.

The Spanish were by far the best. They were the most professional as well as disinterested, and therefore fair.

But then there were the Polish. There was just something about them that was irritating, maybe because they were Polish. I think it also had to do with their anti-Semitic tendencies. Poland had sported high-levels of anti-Semitism for centuries that still existed in modern times. Sometimes when we drove by I started fantasizing about just assaulting their base for no apparent reason. It was a nice thought.

Seeing the United Nations troops was rather weird, though. They cruised around on their side of the border in their white-painted armored vehicles and blue helmets. It was just strange seeing another armed force that was neither enemy nor ally.

Lebanon itself was quite foreign to me as well. It was hard to describe what it was like seeing just on the other side of the fence the flags and political posters of the Hezbollah terrorist organization. Burnt American and Israeli flags littered the ground, and the yellow flag of Islamic terror fluttered high. And it was only a few hundred meters away.

While conducting these patrols we had special technology that emitted a significant amount of radiation. We had to be careful that there was nothing or no one in front of us while operating it. Rumor had it that this device, if on its highest setting, could knock a person to the ground (although I was not totally convinced that this was actually true). The translation of the official name was "Belief." But it didn't take long for it to receive the nickname of "*Blee Neder*," which could be roughly interpreted as "No Guarantees/Promises."

For these patrols we had Druze Arab drivers. The Druze were Arabs living in Israel who were *not* Moslem. The Druze had their own strange and highly secretive religion. So secretive, in fact, that it was impossible to convert to it. A person could only be born into it. Largely for that reason the Druze lacked the conquering-spirit of fanatical Islam that wished to bring all nations to the service of Allah at the point of the sword. But for better or for worse, it also meant that they retained most of the cultural facets of Arabs.

On one patrol we were cruising down along the Lebanese Border in an area known for being more dangerous than most other areas. Suddenly the driver slammed on the brakes and refused to proceed, even turning the Hummer around and high-tailing it back the way we came. An argument proceeded between the Druze Arab driver and Commander Keen (now Sergeant Keen, having replaced Sergeant Obama). The Druze driver refused to explain why he wouldn't proceed. Commander Keen demanded some kind of explanation. Finally, after several full minutes of arguing, the Druze driver finally admitted the problem. The Druze driver refused to proceed because an eighteen year-old girl connected with the field intelligence had called in over the radio that she had seen a rabbit.

And so our heavily-armored Hummer, complete with a mounted .50 caliber machine gun and several elite Paratrooper commanders and designated marksmen, was fleeing in terror.

I was very disappointed. I wanted to use the *Blee Neder* radiation technology on the rabbit. We would soon have had some strange looking bunnies hopping around Lebanon.

Speaking of these field intelligence girls, it amazed me sometimes the attitudes of some soldiers in the Israel Defense Force. On one occasion Captain America was leading a border patrol and began to criticize one of these girls for not doing her job properly. She then shot back in an impudent tone over the radio that he should "say thank you for everything that she actually *did* do." It blew my mind that an eighteen year-old girl sitting in a room and staring at a computer screen would have the *chutzpah* (guts) to say something like that to a twenty-two year-old Paratrooper lieutenant patrolling a potential war zone.

On the Lebanese border I often marveled at the missions presented to us. Occasionally I heard something completely crazy and assumed that I had simply misunderstood due to my imperfect Hebrew. Then I would ask the officer to repeat and clarify.

"I said," Captain America repeated in slower, slightly simpler Hebrew. "That tomorrow we are entering a minefield on foot and that you, Killswitch, are going in first."

"Um, yeah..." I cringed in response. "That's what I thought you said."

As we prepared to go into the minefield Captain America presented to me a two and one-half foot metal rod (about 0.7 meters).

"Do you know what this is for, Killswitch?" He asked as he displayed the stick with connecting handle, almost looking like a very thin cane. "This is for testing mines. If you see something in the minefield that looks suspicious you can take this stick and poke it to see if it blows up."

I looked at Captain America, then at the stick, then back to Captain America. He was out of his mind.[1]

When Israel pulled out of Lebanon completely in 2000 we set up the electronic fence. There were two large hills that were technically ours but still remained on the other side of the fence due to construction difficulties. It was our mission to wander onto these two hills and do a small patrol. But there were a few problems. First off, we had mined the area ourselves. Therefore we needed to make sure to walk only in the area that we hadn't mined. The other problem involved the fact that Hezbollah, who were directly influenced, supplied, and funded by the Syrian and Iranian governments, had quite possibly mined the area as well. Also, the United Nations didn't really like us being there, and Hezbollah didn't like us either, to say the least. It was a very real possibility that a trigger-happy Polish soldier or a Hezbollah sniper or RPG team might come over the other side of the hill and give us a not-so-friendly greeting. It was also my personal task of going in first with a roll of white tape to mark out the trail and make sure it was safe for everybody else.

Gee... Thanks, guys.

We went across the fence into the No Man's Land between Israel and Lebanon. I was surprised just how small the areas were. I wondered what the reaction would have been if only the world knew that often the areas that the Arabs started riots and even wars over were really the size of a couple thousand square meters (yards).

We had a canine unit come with us. The dog had been specially trained to hunt for mines and other explosives. I went in first with the canine soldier. The soldier sent the dog in before us. The dog was wearing a type of vest with a small hand-held radio attached to it. This way the canine soldier communicated to the dog without shouting, whistling, or making any real noise. The dog bounded away onto the hill. It was kind of surreal. The hills were covered with tall, beautiful, yellow wildflowers. It looked like the opening scene from *The*

[1 This really was what the stick was for, i.e., poking suspicious-looking objects in a minefield. The Handasah Kravit (Combat Engineer Battalion) was usually responsible for demining operations. There was a common expression that they only made two mistakes in their lives, and the first was enlisting with the Handasah Kravit.]

Sound of Music. But when Julie Andrews was twirling around in song I doubted that she had any real premonitions about stepping on an explosive device and blowing herself up.

The dog bounced along happily, obviously enjoying his frolic through the flowers. The canine soldier directed him back and forth in his search for mines and weapons. The dog loyally obeyed and conducted himself as if it was all just a big game, anticipating the promised reward of playing with his favorite ball afterward. I shook my head in dismay.

"Stupid dog," I muttered to myself. "He's going to blow his fool self halfway to Beirut and he doesn't even know it."

But then I reconsidered it all. There I was, knowingly walking through a minefield and exposing myself to potential snipers and RPG's. And for what? To make a point to the United Nations and to Hezbollah that these two hills were still ours and we would continue to exercise our right to walk around in circles on them regardless of the landmines? I looked at the large Rottweiler-Shepherd mix. His big, dark brown eyes looked back at me. I was sure that animals could smile in a sense, and he was definitely "smiling" at me. He was content with yellow wildflowers and his favorite ball. And therefore he was happy and had no concerns whatsoever. I looked at the dog, then gazed at Lebanon with all of its political strife, the distant UN armored vehicles watching us and all of the international tensions they represented, my fellow soldiers that I had served with for over two years already and knew better than my own family, the minefield that we had laid and were now walking through for show, and myself.

Maybe the dog wasn't so stupid after all.

July 1st, 2009: Rendezvous with Old Friends and Foes

About this time I completed something called Course Nativ for two months. It was essentially a program for new immigrant soldiers (mostly the Russians) to learn about Jewish history, culture, religion, as wells as Israeli politics. I didn't need the course by any means, but the course was held on a nice campus with delicious food and weekend pass almost every week. Many of my friends also participated, particularly Axl and Lunchbox.

Afterwards they sent me back to the Lebanese Border for a week. I didn't do much. I didn't even sign in for my equipment. Not only did I not sign for new equipment I was able to smuggle out two full "*Bet*" duffel bags of equipment. I was very proud of my own personal armory that I had acquired throughout my military service. Just a few items worthy of note included my custom combat vest, two gas masks, a flak jacket, a sniper camouflage screen, half a dozen sets of uniforms, my boots, numerous battle flags, and of course, my machete` and dagger.

I went back to the Lebanese Border essentially to help them move our base. We were switching our area of operations from the Lebanese Border to Yehudah V' Shomron (the West Bank) near Ramallah. We were moving all of our equipment and practically everything that wasn't nailed down to the ground from the northernmost part of Israel southeast to Yehudah V' Shomron.

They promoted a soldier from the November '07 draft to be a logistics sergeant. This essentially meant that for one day he was supposed to be higher in authority than me. He was just a kid and lower ranking than me. He started his time in the military almost a year after me even. It was ridiculous and even insulting. And he knew it, too. He got himself on a power trip and became a monster. He tried to order me around. I just couldn't take him seriously.

After we spent a few days packing up the base they sent me and Axl to a base in Yehudah V' Shomron (the West Bank). We were supposed to guard the equipment. But there really wasn't much to guard. I spent most of the weekend exploring the nearby caves and archaeological ruins. That was something about Israel. There was so much archeology that much of it wasn't even noticed. Nobody cared. I found the remains of an ancient church built by the Crusaders that was barely even marked. I also explored a set of Sidonian tombs as well as ancient limestone quarries.

By coincidence I ran into one of the South Americans that studied Hebrew with me back on the kibbutz when I first came to Israel. We talked and hung out most of the weekend. It was good to see him and catch up on the latest news with all of our old friends. There had been several marriages and even a few births. Being in the military was almost like dozing off into a Rip Van Winkle-style coma.

Axl and I were later sent to a Paratrooper base near Netanya to sign out all of our remaining equipment. I asked Captain America for permission to go home briefly to retrieve the remainder of my equipment that I needed to turn in. He refused, thinking that we were supposed to return it a different day. Sure enough, I was right. Axl and I found ourselves at the base without our equipment and watching everyone else sign their stuff out. In Captain America's defense it was possible to sign our equipment out at a later date, but that would have involved going home and coming all the way back to the same base. We were already there. Then we came up with a plan. The person in charge of logistics was an Israeli girl who never ceased to be enamored with Americans. Axl went up to her and started flirting around a bit. Meanwhile, I moved over to the pile of checked and turned in equipment and quickly acquired what we needed. I did a circuitous route back and we checked our supplies. Yes, we had it all. Then we turned in "our equipment." She looked at it briefly and then said, "Okay, you see that pile of equipment over there? Put these bags over there." I almost replied, "You mean the pile where I got them from?" But I thought that would have been pushing my luck. On the plus side all of my equipment that I had elsewhere was now mine to keep.

On the base in Netanya I ran into WD-40, the American who had immigrated with his family and had dropped out of combat because of his health situation. He had been so promiscuous that he had developed a nasty STD. In the end they had to subject him to some kind of extremely painful laser treatment. He claimed to have gone on a religious revival of sorts, and even began criticizing me for my dating life. The hypocrisy was astounding.

Then Axl and I went on a short "End of Service" Tour in the army. They sent us with the August '06 draft. That wasn't our draft but that was fine. We goofed around the Galil and the Golan Heights for two and a half days. Then we returned to the base in Netanya. We had a small dinner and ceremony. Major Bloodlust and the colonel presented us with our framed certificates that we had officially finished our service in the Israel Defense Force. With a little bit of luck and a lot of begging I got a ride back to my kibbutz and was back at home, now a free man, at about two in the morning.

By happy coincidence Rocky-Roodle, my girl from Great Britain, came back to Israel the day I was released from the army. She and her brothers decided to do a three week tour in Israel. Obviously it wasn't long before we got back together.

She stopped by the kibbutz to visit me the day after I was released. She had left her cell phone with her brothers and was unsure of where my new apartment was. When she arrived she went to the *cheder ochel* (dining room). She saw some volunteer girls and assumed that they knew me.

"Excuse me," Rocky-Roodle began. "I'm here to see Killswitch. Do you know where he is?"

The entire table of girls (consisting exclusively of recipients of the infamous April Fool's multiple love letter) stared in disgust and sneered at her.

"Um... okay. What's the matter? Don't you like him?" Rocky-Roodle asked innocently.

"Well, we *did* like him..." One of them scowled without explanation.

My active service in the Israel Defense Force was officially over and I was now part of the Special Forces Battalion Reserves, Jerusalem Brigade. I gave almost three years of my life for Israel and the Jewish people. I almost died for Israel. They even pronounced me dead over the radio in Operation: Cast Lead. I received absolutely no personal benefit from any of that. And that was perfectly fine. I was happy about what I had done and my service to Israel.

I sat on the edge of the bed, feeling rather lazy after having slept in until ten in the morning. I thought about everything I did in the last three years. I thought about the decisions I had made, how hard I had worked, the people I had met, the people I had killed, and all of my successes as well as failures. Was I sorry? Did I regret any of it?

No.

I was not saying that all of my experiences had been pleasant. But I knew that I had made the right choice. I didn't know what would become of me in the future. I didn't know what would become of the friends I had made. I didn't know what would become of the enemies I had created. I gazed over at Rocky-Roodle sleeping peacefully. I didn't know what would happen with us. I leaned over to kiss her sleeping mouth gently. She slowly stirred awake.

I lay down next to her, gently stroking her back with my fingertips. I had been thinking about us for a while now. Rocky-Roodle was definitely a very special person. I thought about the different directions our lives would be taking us in the near future. I also realized more than ever that I didn't want to lose her. I remembered that my friend had recommended a jewelry shop in central Jerusalem. Maybe it was time to buy her a ring.

Rocky-Roodle soon woke up and we began to discuss plans for Shabbat since it was already Friday morning. Our mutual friend from Finland, Boots, would be visiting us this weekend. I made a stupid joke, as was my custom of doing at least twenty-seven times a day. She visibly tensed and rose from the bed.

"I've put up with enough, Killswitch," Rocky-Roodle declared with a fabricated resolve that I could tell wasn't really there. I sat on the bed in shock, knowing what was coming but unable to believe it.

"I can't do this anymore," she continued with her voice breaking and her back turned to me. "Although you have always been so nice to me, you've never cheated on me, you've always taken care of me, and you've always cared about my needs, but... I've put up with enough."

Nothing she said made any sense to me, or to anyone else for that matter. She turned around. She didn't expect to see what she saw.

I sat on the edge of the bed, broken, with tears silently falling down my face. She had never seen me cry before. Could this possible? Me, the fearless Paratrooper, the combat veteran, the cold-blooded killer, the arrogant braggart, the smooth talker, the ingenious prankster, the popular American, in tears? I felt vulnerable and therefore became angry and confused. And in that moment I made perhaps the greatest mistake of my life:

I let Rocky-Roodle go.

I had fought for my ideals, for my nation, for my people, and for my friends. I had stared the Angel of Death in the face and survived. But now it was the time to fight for her, for us, for myself. And I allowed myself to be defeated. When Rocky-Roodle walked out of my apartment that final time I never saw her again.

PART X: CONCLUSION

Conclusion: Mazal Tov and a Moment of Silence

Not long after I finished my military service in the Israel Defense Force I found myself in Europe, supposedly on a brief tour with Lunchbox. I stood in front of an old hotel, sweltering from the Mediterranean humidity. I adjusted my constricting bright blue tie, which was the prearranged signal. A few minutes later a black BMW station wagon pulled up in front of the hotel. Out stepped several individuals I had never seen before but had been apprehensively waiting to meet. I emerged from the backdrop and approached them. They greeted me in a professional manner and I slid into the backseat. The driver immediately pulled out of the parking lot. In more ways than one I was unsure of the destination. It was then that I realized that this wasn't the end of my adventures. It was only the beginning.

Almost a year after Rocky-Roodle broke up with me, Boots, our mutual Finnish friend, admitted to me the *real* reason behind it all. Everyone knew it wasn't because I had made yet another stupid joke. But I wasn't prepared for what I was told.

Apparently Rocky-Roodle broke up with me because she had come to the conclusion that I had no intention of ever becoming more serious with her. Boots confessed that largely due to her own horrifically bad advice Rocky-Roodle simply mustered up an excuse to leave me. She ended the relationship on her terms because she thought that would be better for her emotionally in the long run.

Rocky-Roodle had no idea how much I cared about her, indeed, loved her. She was completely oblivious to the fact that I was looking at rings to buy her. She was totally unaware of any of it. She honestly thought that when the time came I would send her on her way and forget about her. And that was why she was so shocked to see my tears when she left me.

I now had to face the fact that the breakup was completely pointless and had been the result of a severe lack of communication on both our parts and extremely foolish counsel from her friends. We both had refused to tell each other how we really felt and what we really wanted for the future, even when we both knew we would lose it all.

But at this point in time it was already too late. I had taken on a set of career projects that took me away from Israel for the time being, even though I would always consider Israel to be my home. Likewise, she had already entered into a serious relationship with someone else. There was realistically nothing I could do about the situation. I had no interest in being vicious and cruel and attempting to destroy her current relationship. Even then her happiness was still paramount to me. And I wasn't in Israel consistently enough to rekindle a relationship with her even if she was single. She never learned how close she came to getting a ring from me. She still lives with the misconception that we had no future.

Every once in a while one of her friends would criticize me for the breakup, obviously knowing little to nothing of the events and circumstances around them. One of her roommates even publicly called me "evil." I was highly offended by their *chutzpah*, judging a person they hardly knew for a situation they had no real knowledge of. Besides that, it wasn't any of their business anyway. But I always quietly bore the ridicule and simply walked away.

I never told Rocky-Roodle the truth about it all. Not for my sake, but for hers.

Somewhere deep inside I knew that Rocky-Roodle would never have been happy with me. (In fact, I had my doubts that she was *ever* truly happy with me.) I had now immersed myself in a vicious world full of intrigue and treachery. A world of death and betrayal. A world in which I would forever sit in the corner seat of the local café with my back to the wall and watch the entrance. A world in which I carried weapons with me at all times. A world in which I would walk down the street and glance at the reflection in car mirrors out of the corner of my eye to make sure no one was following me. A world in which my associates and I would nurse our beers and quietly relate tales of the people we had killed. A world in which every day we would gamble with the ultimate stakes: our very lives. And why did I feel compelled to enter such a world and pursue such a career? Because, unfortunately, I was very good at it.

I wasn't a fool. I would never admit it to anyone but I was secretly convinced that if Rocky-Roodle had married me she would have been miserable and eventually divorced me.

At some later point I discovered that Rocky-Roodle's serious relationship with this other unknown individual resulted in marriage. And not long after she gave birth to a beautiful baby girl.[1] I wished them well. At least with him she had a chance to be happy.

Mazal tov and a moment of silence.

[1 I will refrain from giving Rocky-Roodle's baby a ridiculous nickname.]

Maybe one day I would tell her I was sorry. Maybe one day, but not today...

... My body slammed into the asphalt and I continued to slide across the highway. Eventually I came to a stop and became aware of my surroundings. I lay flat on my back as the sounds of screeching tires, blaring horns, and crunching metal filled my ears as if from some far away place. I sat up and noted several onlookers staring at me with wide eyes. With an audible grunt I pulled myself to my feet and limped my way over twenty feet (six meters) back to my motorcycle. Despite the violence of the crash, the damage to The Pale Horse was oddly minimal. By myself I lifted the 450 pound (200 kilogram) motorcycle upright and began to clear out the flooded carburetors. At some point someone would comment, "Hey, are you the Terminator or something?" I ignored him and started up the bike. Not having hit anything myself, I climbed onto the bike and continued down the highway.[1]

Soreness began to enter my muscles as I continued to ride. More than that, I tried to shake the effects of the flashback from my mind. With a heavy sigh I kicked The Pale Horse into top gear and twisted the handle to accelerate the motorbike. Reminiscing of a distant time when my only concerns were making the most of my weekend leave from the Israel Defense Force and enjoying the time spent with the beautiful British girl in my arms I rode off into the Arizona sunset, realizing that those days would never come again.

[1 At this point I had taken a temporary job to keep up my cash flow. In spite of the crash I limped into work only seven minutes late. Regardless, my boss actually wrote me up for being tardy. Not long afterwards I quit and told him off with a few choice words in several languages, many of which had been learned from my fellow Lone Soldiers in the IDF. I realized more than ever that I would never be happy in the civilian work-force and that "normal" jobs were simply not the best utilization of my talents and abilities. Instead I shifted all of my focus to a series of both domestic and international security and training projects.]

Made in the USA
Charleston, SC
16 March 2013